Hannes Gumtau
Wolfgang Kurschatke

Grammatik im Lernsystem Band 3

ab 3. Lernjahr

MANZ VERLAG

Mit neuer deutscher Rechtschreibung

4. verbesserte Auflage 1999
Manz Verlag
© Ernst Klett Verlag GmbH, Stuttgart 1989
Alle Rechte vorbehalten
Umschlaggestaltung: Zembsch' Werkstatt, München
Illustrationen: Gisela Gumtau, Schongau
Gesamtherstellung: Verlag und Druckerei G. J. Manz AG, München/Dillingen
Printed in Germany

ISBN 3-7863-0546-3

INHALT

3

SCHWERPUNKTE DER SCHULAUFGABEN (= Klassenarbeiten)   159

SYSTEMATISCH LERNEN

Liebe Schülerin, lieber Schüler!

Grammatik im Lernsystem hilft dir beim Erlernen und Wiederholen der englischen Grammatik. Die Aufgaben beziehen sich immer auf einen bestimmten Schwerpunkt, sodass du zielstrebig üben kannst.
Auf Bildergeschichten und Situationen verzichten wir bewusst, weil du diese in deinem Lehrbuch und Workbook zur Genüge vorfindest und du dich auf das **Wesentliche der Grammatik** konzentrieren sollst.

Grammatik im Lernsystem ermöglicht dir systematisches Lernen:

1. Der Grammatikstoff der ersten Lernjahre ist in 12 Kapitel unterteilt: Symbole **A–M.**

2. In diesem Band übst du die **Schwerpunkte des 3. Lernjahres.**

3. Das **Lernsystem** auf den Seiten 8 bis 11 zeigt dir, wie du konsequent alle Schwerpunkte **wiederholen** kannst.

4. Du musst diesen Band keineswegs von Anfang bis Ende durcharbeiten. Suche dir deine persönlichen Themen.
Notiere dir, was bei der nächsten **Schulaufgabe** (oder: Klassenarbeit, Extemporale, Nachprüfung) verlagt wird, und suche die entsprechenden Aufgaben heraus.

5. Als spezielles **Prüfungstraining** findest du auf den Seiten 159 bis 189 10 **Schulaufgaben,** die du gezielt einsetzen kannst. Suche dir jeweils die für dich wichtigen Aufgaben, indem du die Schwerpunkte auf Seite 6 überprüfst.

6. Auf Seite 12 findest du ein Muster für deine **Lernstrategie.**

Wir wünschen dir viel Erfolg!

DAS LERNSYSTEM	SCHWERPUNKTE DER GRAMMATIK IM BAND 1
A◀ **Artikel Substantiv**	● a / an ● the [ðə] [ði] ● this / these – that / those ● Regelmäßige Pluralbildung ● Unregelmäßige Pluralbildung ● Der s-Genitiv ● Der of-Genitiv
B◀ **Zahlen Mengen- bezeichnungen**	● Die Grundzahlen ● Die Ordnungszahlen ● some – any
C◀ **Pronomen**	● Die Personalpronomen ● Die adjektivisch gebrauchten Possessivpronomen (my, your, . . .)
D◀ **Adjektiv Adverb**	
E◀ **Verb: Gegenwart**	● 'to be' ● 'to have' ● Das Present Progressive ● Das Simple Present ● Der verneinte Satz ● Gegenüberstellung von Present Progressive und Simple Present
F◀ **Verb: Vergangenheit**	

SCHWERPUNKTE DER GRAMMATIK IM BAND 2	SCHWERPUNKTE DER GRAMMATIK IM BAND 3
● Wiederholung: a / an, the ● Der bestimmte Artikel in Sonderfällen ● Wiederholung: s-Genitiv of-Genitiv	● Wiederholung: regelmäßiger und unregelmäßiger Plural ● Substantive nur im Singular ● Substantive nur im Plural ● Der s-Genitiv bei Zeitangaben ● Der s-Genitiv bei Ortsangaben
● Wiederholung: some – any ● some bei Aufforderung oder Angebot ● some, any und ihre Zusammensetzungen ● a lot of – much / many – a few / a little	● Wiederholung: some, any und ihre Zusammensetzungen ● every – each – any
● Wiederholung: Personalpronomen und adjektivisch gebrauchte Possessivpronomen ● Die substantivisch gebrauchten Possessivpronomen (mine, yours, . . .)	● Wiederholung: Personalpronomen und Possessivpronomen ● Die Reflexivpronomen (myself, . . .) ● Die reziproken Pronomen (each other, one another)
● Die Steigerung der Adjektive ● Der Vergleich im Satz ● Die Bildung des Adverbs (politely) ● Der Unterschied im Gebrauch von Adjektiv und Adverb ● Das Stützwort one	● Wiederholung: Adjektiv und Adverb ● Adjektiv nach bestimmten Verben ● Gleiche Form von Adjektiv und Adverb (fast) ● Adverbien mit zwei Formen (hard / hardly) ● Die Steigerung des Adverbs
● Wiederholung: Present Progressive und Simple Present ● Das Simple Present bei bestimmten Verben (know, belong to, . . .)	● Wiederholung: Present Progressive und Simple Present
● Das Simple Past ● Die Verneinung des Simple Past ● Das Present Perfect ● Gegenüberstellung von Simple Past und Present Perfect ● Das Past Progressive	● Wiederholung: Past und Present Perfect ● Das Present Perfect Progressive ● Das Past Perfect

DAS LERNSYSTEM	SCHWERPUNKTE DER GRAMMATIK IM BAND 1
G‹ **Verb: Zukunft**	
H‹ **Verb: Andere Formen**	
I‹ **Modale Hilfsverben**	● Can – Can't ● Must – Needn't
K‹ **Satzgefüge**	
L‹ **Fragesätze**	● Yes- / No-Fragen ● W-Fragen ● Subjektfragen ● Verneinte Fragen
M‹ **Wortstellung**	● Der einfache englische Satz ● Häufigkeitsadverbien (often) ● Adverbien des Ortes und der Zeit (at school, at five o'clock)

SCHWERPUNKTE DER GRAMMATIK IM BAND 2	SCHWERPUNKTE DER GRAMMATIK IM BAND 3
● Das going to-Future ● Das will-Future ● Gegenüberstellung von going to-Future und will-Future	● Wiederholung: going to-Future und will-Future ● Das Future Progressive ● Das Future Perfect ● Das 'Present Progressive' Future
	● Das Passiv ● Die -ing Form (Gerund) ● Der Infinitiv nach Fragewörtern (how to, when to . . .) ● Der Infinitiv nach Adjektiven ● Objekt + Infinitiv mit to
● Wiederholung: Can – Can't ● May ● Can – able to / allowed to ● Wiederholung: Must – Needn't ● Mustn't ● Must – have to	● Wiederholung: Can, Must, May ● Can – Could ● May – Might ● Will – Would ● Should – Ought to
	● Bedingungssätze (= If-Sätze): Typ 1 ● Bedingungssätze (= If-Sätze): Typ 2 ● Bedingungssätze (= If-Sätze): Typ 3 ● Relativsätze ● Die indirekte Rede
● Wiederholung: Fragebildung in der Gegenwart ● Fragebildung: Past Tense ● Fragebildung: Present Perfect und Future ● Question tags	● Wiederholung: Fragebildung in allen Zeiten ● Fragebildung mit nachgestellten Präpositionen (What are you looking at?)
● Wiederholung: Satzbau (Grundmuster) ● Adverbien der Art und Weise (slowly) ● Gradadverbien (extremely)	● Wiederholung: Satzbau (Grundmuster) ● Verben mit zwei Objekten (direktes und indirektes Objekt)

Muster für deine **Lernstrategie**:

1. Für meine nächste Arbeit muss ich folgende **Schwerpunkte** üben:

_____   _____

_____   _____

_____   _____

☐

2. Dazu bearbeite ich folgende **Aufgaben:**
(Du gehst das Inhaltsverzeichnis auf den Seiten 3 bis 5 durch bzw. informierst dich auf den Seiten 8 bis 11, ob du frühere Schwerpunkte wiederholen müsstest.)

Seite _____   Seite _____   Seite _____

_____   _____   _____

_____   _____   _____

☐

3. Zur **Lernzielkontrolle** vergleiche ich meine Antworten mit den Vorschlägen im Lösungsheft.

☐

4. Als gezieltes **Prüfungstraining** bearbeite ich dann folgende **Schulaufgaben** (oder Teile von Schulaufgaben).
(Du suchst deine Schwerpunkte aus den 10 Aufgaben auf Seite 6 heraus.)

☐

5. Du vergleichst auch jetzt mit den Angaben im Lösungsheft.

☐

6. Du löst als Zusammenfassung des Lernstoffes die entsprechenden Aufgaben des **Grammatikquiz** auf den Seiten 155 bis 158. Die Antworten lernst du **auswendig.**

☐

SCHWERPUNKTE
DER GRAMMATIK

Bei allen Übungen ist in Kursivdruck rechts oben angegeben, wo die jeweilige Grammatik im Tafelbild erklärt wird (z. B. *Lernhilfen auf Seite 14*).

Denke an die Symbole:

● = Schwerpunkt eines Kapitels

● = Merkpunkt zum Auswendiglernen

Die grau unterlegten Teile der Tafelbilder sind Wiederholungen aus Band 1 und Band 2. Die blau unterlegten Teile sind der neue Lernstoff. Präge dir die Beispiele und Wörter ein und hake sie ab, wenn du sie sicher beherrschst, z. B. $\boxed{\text{V}}$.

Artikel – Substantiv

 Regelmäßige und unregelmäßige Pluralbildung
Wiederholung aus Band 1, Seiten 16 und 17

Regelmäßiger Plural
(= regular plural):

☐ shop → shop**s**

● Du hängst **-s** an die Singularform des Substantivs an.

☐ tomato → tomato**es**

☐ piano → piano**s**

● Bei einigen Substantiven auf -o (tomato, potato, negro) schreibst du **-es,** bei anderen (piano, radio, disco, kilo, photo, studio) **-s.**

☐ beach → beach**es**

☐ brush → brush**es**

☐ fox → fox**es**

☐ boss → boss**es**

● Bei Substantiven, die auf Zischlaut enden (-ch, -sh, -x, -ss), hängst du immer **-es** an.

☐ shelf → shel**ves**

☐ life → li**ves**

☐ roof → roof**s**

● Bei vielen Substantiven auf -f oder -fe ist der Plural **-ves** (shelf, life, wife, knife, calf), bei anderen **-s** (roof, proof, chief).

☐ country → countr**ies**

☐ trolley → trolley**s**

● Bei Substantiven auf -y bildest du den Plural mit **-ies,** wenn vor dem -y ein Konsonant steht (z. B. country), sonst hängst du **-s** an.

Unregelmäßiger Plural
(= irregular plural):

☐ man → m**e**n

☐ policewoman → policewom**e**n

● Die besonderen Formen musst du stets wiederholen.

1.

Lernhilfen auf Seite 14

Fill in the singular or plural of the words in brackets.
(Verwende die Wörter in der Klammer in der Einzahl oder Mehrzahl.)

a) On _____ (Saturday) all the _____ (shop)

   are open, but the _____ (school) are closed.

b) The _____ (boy) and _____ (girl) need not go to

   _____ (school).

c) Some _____ (man) and _____ (woman) must work at

   _____ (weekend).

d) On a _____ (weekday) we can buy a lot of _____

   (thing) at the _____ (shop) in our town.

e) At the market we can buy _____ (potato),

   _____ (tomato), _____ (apple), _____

   (peach), _____ (plum), _____ (carrot), _____

   (strawberry) and many other _____ (thing).

f) The _____ (child) can help their _____
   (parent) at home.

g) In the garden they can plant all _____ (sort) of _____

   (vegetable) or wonderful _____ (flower) or they can

   play hide-and-seek behind the _____ (bush) and _____

   (tree) with their _____ (friend).

Substantive nur im Singular

☐ knowledge	=	*Kenntnis, Kenntnisse*
☐ news	=	*Nachricht, Nachrichten*
☐ advice	=	*Rat, Ratschläge*
☐ information	=	*Information, Informa-* *tionen*
☐ furniture	=	*Möbel*
☐ progress	=	*Fortschritt, Fortschritte*
☐ homework	=	*Hausaufgabe, Haus-* *aufgaben*

● Einige Substantive
(= nouns) haben im Eng-
lischen **nur** die **Singular-**
form.

☐ My knowledge of English is good.
Meine Englischkenntnisse sind gut.

☐ This news sounds good.
Diese Nachrichten klingen gut.

● Die zugeordneten Verben
(z. B. is, sounds) und die
Bestimmungswörter
(z. B. this) stehen eben-
falls im **Singular.**

☐ furniture	=	*Möbel*
☐ a piece of furniture	=	*ein Möbelstück*
☐ some pieces of furniture	=	*ein paar Möbel*
☐ advice	=	*Rat, Ratschläge*
☐ a piece of advice	=	*ein Rat*

● Wenn du eine bestimmte
Anzahl angeben willst,
kannst du **piece** davor
setzen.

2.

Lernhilfen auf Seite 16

Translate into English. (Übersetze ins Englische.)

a) Billy hat schlechte Kenntnisse in Geographie.

_____

b) Tony macht in der Schule gute Fortschritte.

_____

c) Hat Sally ihre Hausaufgaben schon gemacht?

_____

d) Die Informationen über das Treffen sind sehr wichtig.

_____

e) Der Doktor gab Tom einen guten Rat.

_____

f) Die Möbel in unserem Haus sind sehr alt.

_____

g) Meine Tante schenkte uns letztes Jahr ein paar Möbel.

_____

_____

h) Ein Sessel ist ein Möbelstück, auf dem man sitzen kann.

_____

_____

i) Die Auskünfte, die Peter mir gab, waren falsch.

_____

Substantive nur im Plural

☐ trousers	=	*Hose, Hosen*
☐ shorts	=	*kurze Hose*
☐ jeans	=	*Jeans*
☐ tights	=	*Strumpfhose, Strumpfhosen*
☐ scissors	=	*Schere, Scheren*
☐ glasses	=	*Brille, Brillen*
☐ stairs	=	*Treppe, Treppen*
☐ outskirts	=	*Außenbezirk, Außenbezirke*
☐ pyjamas	=	*Schlafanzug, Schlafanzüge*

● Einige Substantive (= nouns), z. B. Wörter für zweiteilige oder mehrteilige Dinge, haben **nur** die **Plural**form.

☐ These trousers are new.
Diese Hose ist neu.

☐ Those scissors don't cut.
Jene Schere schneidet nicht.

● Die zugeordneten Verben (z. B. are, don't) und die Bestimmungswörter (z. B. these, those) stehen ebenfalls im **Plural**.

☐ trousers	=	*Hose, Hosen*
☐ a pair of trousers	=	*ein Paar Hosen*
☐ two pairs of trousers	=	*zwei Paar Hosen*

● Wenn du eine genaue **Anzahl** angeben willst, stellst du **pair/pairs** voran.

3.

Translate into English. (Übersetze ins Englische.)

a) Bills Hose ist sehr schmutzig.

_____

b) Er braucht eine neue Hose.

_____

c) Jane trägt eine Brille.

_____

d) Sie kann ihre Brille nicht finden.

_____

e) Diese Schere ist nicht sehr scharf.

_____

f) Ich möchte zwei gute Scheren kaufen.

_____

g) Diese Strumpfhose ist zu groß.

_____

h) Ich brauche eine neue Strumpfhose, zwei kurze Hosen, drei Hemden und einen Schlafanzug.

_____

_____

i) Mein Freund lebt im Außenbezirk von London.

_____

j) Vielen Dank für deinen Brief.

_____

● Der s-Genitiv bei Zeitangaben

an hour's walk   *ein einstündiger Spaziergang*   ☐

today's newspaper   *die heutige Zeitung*   ☐

● Du verwendest den **s-Genitiv** (= s-genitive) auch bei **Zeitangaben.**
● Wie beim s-Genitiv bei Personen gilt:
's beim **Singular** – an hour's walk (wie: a boy's bike)

● Der s-Genitiv bei Ortsangaben

1
London's Underground   *Londons Untergrundbahn*   ☐

Britain's history   *die Geschichte Britanniens*   ☐

to the baker's   *zur Bäckerei, zum Bäcker*   ☐

2
at the butcher's   *in der Metzgerei, beim Metzger*   ☐

at my aunt's   *bei meiner Tante (zu Hause)*   ☐

St Paul's   *die St.-Pauls-Kathedrale*   ☐

● Der **s-Genitiv** (= s-genitive) steht auch bei [1]**Ortsangaben.**

● In zahlreichen Wendungen bleibt der [2]**Ort** ungenannt:
to the baker's (shop), at the butcher's (shop), at my aunt's (house), St Paul's (Cathedral).

4.

Lernhilfen auf Seite 20

Complete the sentences. (Vervollständige die Sätze.)

a) Please bring me _____ (today, paper).

b) Tom worked hard and then he had _____ (an hour, rest).

c) Mr Barber went to _____ (the newsagent) to buy

_____ (this week, magazine).

d) After a _____ (month, wait) the

the book they had ordered arrived at _____ (their uncle).

e) Mary buys some milk and vegetables at _____ (the grocer)

and then she goes to _____ (the butcher) to
get some meat.

f) At _____ (Foyle) you can buy any book you want and at

_____ (Woolworth) you will find nearly any
kind of clothes.

g) You can see _____ (today, weather
forecast) at six o'clock.

h) After a hard _____ (day, work), Mr Copper
arrived home very late.

i) Mrs Short had to buy some medicine at _____ (the chemist).

5.

Lernhilfen auf Seite 20

Translate into English. (Übersetze ins Englische.)

a) Lisa kauft Obst beim Gemüsehändler und Brot beim Bäcker.

_____

_____

b) Laura verbringt eine Woche Ferien bei ihrem Onkel in Wales.

_____

_____

c) Das ist die gestrige Zeitung. Hast du die heutige gesehen?

_____

_____

d) Die Familie Smith macht jeden Sonntag einen einstündigen Spaziergang.

_____

_____

e) Du kannst das Heft beim Schreibwarenhändler kaufen.

_____

_____

f) Um Himmels willen, Johnny, du musst zum Friseur gehen. Deine Haare sind zu lang.

_____

_____

6.

Dictation (Diktat: Wähle die richtige Form.)

Jennifer Hall and her _____ (parent's, parents) have

arranged to go to the _____ (Scottish, scottish)

Highlands for a _____ (weeks, week's)

holiday. The brochures they've sent for are very promising with lovely mountains,

_____ (beautifull, beautiful) lakes

and _____ (island's, islands). Unfortunately, most of

the camping _____ (sites, sights) the _____

(advertisments, advertisements) offered are still closed. This is not so dis-

appointing, because Jennifer has made an excellent suggestion: 'Why don't we go

to a caravan camp?' _____ (Their, There)

are _____ (childrens', childrens, children's) playgrounds

and amusement _____ (arcade's, arcades) for young

_____ (peoples, people's) and _____

(parents, parents') entertainment. I suppose the camp is _____

(quiet, quite) near a town, so we can make a sight-seeing tour with a guide. I can

go to a disco, and Mum to the _____ (grocers,

grocer's) to buy some food. Honestly, we'll enjoy _____

(ourself, ourselves) a lot and our holiday will be a great success.

23

B

Zahlen – Mengenbezeichnungen

7.

Fill in 'some' or 'any' or their compounds.
(Setze 'some' oder 'any' oder ihre Zusammensetzungen ein.)

a) Tina: Has _____ seen my bike? I can't find it

             _____ .

      Anne: No, I haven't. It must be _____ in the garage

             or _____ has taken it.

b) Tina: Have you seen Judy _____? I must tell her

             _____ .

      Anne: Yes, I have. She went to town with _____ I don't

             know. Perhaps they are doing _____ shopping.

c) Tina: Have you got _____ idea where Mr Parker lives?

      Anne: No, _____ of us knows that. I think he lives

             _____ near the river.

d) Tina: May I have _____ more coffee, please?

      Anne: Yes, of course. I'll go to the kitchen to make _____ more.

             Would you like _____ biscuits?

      Tina: Yes, please. I haven't eaten _____ for

             _____ weeks.

● Every – each – any

Every house has windows.

Jedes Haus hat Fenster. ☐

Each of the houses over there has a red roof.

Jedes der Häuser dort drüben hat eine rote Tür. ☐

You can come **any** time.

Du kannst zu jeder (beliebigen) Zeit kommen. ☐

- ● Das deutsche **jede, jeder, jedes** heißt im Englischen **every** oder **each.**
- ● **Every** bedeutet ganz allgemein **jeder** (jeder ohne Ausnahme)
- ● **Each** heißt **jeder von** ... (jeder aus einer bestimmten Anzahl).
- ● **Any** heißt im Aussagesatz **jeder** (beliebige), **irgendeiner** oder **ganz gleich welcher.**

Merke dir die Zusammensetzungen:

everyone
everybody } = *jeder, alle, jedermann* ☐

everything = *alles* ☐
everywhere = *überall* ☐

25

B

8. *Lernhilfen auf Seite 25*
Fill in every, everyone, everything, everywhere, each or any. (Setze ein.)

a) Today ist Mary's birthday. She has a party _____ year.

b) She has invited _____ girl in her class.

c) At five o'clock _____ has been prepared and Mary has

a last look into _____ room.

d) There are flowers _____ and _____ of the

boys who arrives gets a red one and _____ of the girls a blue
one.

e) _____ of her friends brings a present.

f) Mary's mother asks: "Is _____ all right, or do you
need more chairs?"

g) Mary answers: "Thank you, Mum. I've put chairs _____

so I think _____ can enjoy the dinner.

_____ of us has got room enough at the tables.

I told my friends that they could come _____ time they want."

h) _____ dances and they are all in a good mood.

i) _____ boy and _____ girl can learn to dance.

9.

Lernhilfen auf Seite 25

Translate into English. (Übersetze ins Englische.)

a) Jeder Schüler in unserer Klasse mag Englisch.

_____

b) Jedes Auto braucht ein Nummernschild.

_____

c) Du kannst diese Reklame überall sehen.

_____

d) Jeder in unserem Haus ist sehr nett.

_____

e) Habt ihr alles verstanden?

_____

f) Jeder von uns kennt den neuen Film.

_____

g) Jede beliebige Person in unserem Klub kann den Platz benützen.

_____

_____

h) Ich bin sicher, dass jedes Kind gerne Ball spielt.

_____

i) Wir sahen, wie jemand im Fluss schwamm.

_____

j) Du hättest jeden von ihnen fragen können.

_____

k) Ist noch etwas Essen da? – Nein, die Jungen haben alles aufgegessen.

_____

_____

Pronomen

Personalpronomen und Possessivpronomen
Wiederholung aus Band 1, Seiten 37, 41, und Band 2, Seite 32

10.

Fill in the missing pronouns. (Setze die fehlenden Pronomen ein.)

a) John: _____ bike is being repaired, could _____ lend ____ ____, Bob?

   Bob: Yes, of course. _____ don't need _____ this week. _____

   could also use _____ father's.

b) Mary: Did _____ post _____ letters yesterday?

   Anne: Yes, _____ did, but _____ forgot to post _____.

c) John to Diane: _____ can use _____ pencil if _____ don't find _____.

d) Mary to Jane: _____ house is more modern than _____. We built it last year.

e) Mother: Where are _____ glasses?

   Father: _____ haven't seen _____. _____ think _____ put

   _____ in _____ handbag, but if _____ can't find

   _____ _____ can take _____.

f) Mrs Spice: Whose boots are those? Are _____ _____, John?

   John: Yes, _____ are _____. _____ forgot to take

   _____ into the house yesterday.

Die Reflexivpronomen

Formen

I see	**myself**	*ich sehe*	mich	☐
you see	**yourself**	*du siehst*	dich	☐
he sees	**himself**	*er sieht*	sich	☐
she sees	**herself**	*sie sieht*	sich	☐
it sees	**itself**	*es sieht*	sich	☐
we see	**ourselves**	*wir sehen*	uns	☐
you see	**yourselves**	*ihr seht*	euch	☐
they see	**themselves**	*sie sehen*	sich	☐

● Die **Reflexivpronomen** (= reflexive pronouns, self-pronouns) sind Zusammensetzungen mit **-self** (im Singular) bzw. **-selves** (im Plural).

● Unterscheide **yourself** (= dich) und **yourselves** (= euch).

Anwendung

I see **myself** in the mirror.

Susan hurt **herself.**

We enjoyed **ourselves** very much.

● Hier wird das Reflexivpronomen **reflexiv** gebraucht, d. h. **rückbezüglich.** Das Subjekt (z. B. I, Susan, we) bezieht die Handlung auf sich selbst.

The boys made the boat **themselves.**

We saw the king **himself.**

We drew the picture **ourselves.**

● Hier dient das Reflexivpronomen zur **Hervorhebung** von Substantiven (z. B. the boys, the king) oder Pronomen (z. B. we). Man nennt es dann **verstärkendes Pronomen** (= emphasizing pronoun).

29

Unterschiede zum Deutschen:

We meet	every Friday.
Wir treffen uns	*jeden Freitag.*
I can't	remember.
Ich kann	*mich nicht erinnern.*

● Viele im Deutschen reflexive Verben sind im Englischen **nicht-reflexive Verben,** d. h., **sich** wird nicht übersetzt.

Merke dir:

☐ to apologize	= *sich entschuldigen*
☐ to approach	= *sich nähern*
☐ to be afraid (of)	= *sich fürchten*
☐ to be angry	= *sich ärgern*
☐ to be interested (in)	= *sich interessieren*
☐ to change	= *sich ändern*
☐ to concentrate	= *sich konzentrieren*
☐ to differ (from)	= *sich unterscheiden*
☐ to fall in love	= *sich verlieben*
☐ to feel	= *sich fühlen*
☐ to get used to	= *sich gewöhnen an*
☐ to happen	= *sich ereignen*
☐ to imagine	= *sich einbilden*
☐ to join	= *sich anschließen*
☐ to lie down	= *sich hinlegen*
☐ to meet	= *sich treffen*
☐ to move	= *sich bewegen*
☐ to prove	= *sich erweisen*
☐ to quarrel	= *sich streiten*
☐ to refuse	= *sich weigern*
☐ to remember	= *sich erinnern (an)*
☐ to rise	= *sich erheben*
☐ to sit down	= *sich setzen*
☐ to wonder	= *sich fragen*

11.

Lernhilfen auf Seiten 29, 30

Fill in the correct form of 'oneself'. (Setze die richtige Form von 'oneself' ein.)

a) Tom cut _____ with a knife.

b) Barbara hurt _____ when she fell down the stairs.

c) Mary and Clara were pleased with _____.

d) My friend Bob enjoyed _____ at the party yesterday.

e) Paul, you must look after _____.

f) The dog was scratching _____ behind the ear.

g) Can't you repair your car _____, Tom?

h) Many housewives don't want to do all the work _____.

i) The new girl introduced _____ to the teacher.

j) Anne told me that she had painted the picture _____.

k) "Help _____ at the counter of the self-service restaurant", Peter said to his friends.

l) My brother bought _____ a bicycle last summer.

m) The old man is always talking to _____.

n) Can I help you? – No, thanks. We can do the work _____.

o) Ian and Jean taught _____ how to ride a horse.

p) Who took these nice photos, Charles? – Oh, I took them all by _____ .

12.

Lernhilfen auf Seiten 29, 30

Fill in the reflexive pronoun, if necessary.

(Setze das Reflexivpronomen ein, wenn es notwendig ist.)

a) Do you remember _____ my friend Chris?

   – Yes, I do. I've been asking _____ what he does in his
free time.

   – Chris has joined _____ a group of young people.

b) The group meets _____ every Friday night.

c) They amuse _____ with films or dancing.

d) One evening Chris was late and so he apologized _____.

e) The reason was that he had to wash _____ and dress

_____ before he went to the meeting.

f) This evening the young people wondered _____ what they could
do next Saturday.

g) One of them asked: "Do you think we can do all the preparations

_____?"

h) Chris says: "We could have a barbecue. I organised one last month all by

_____."

i) At the barbecue the guests can help _____ to some drinks
and the food.

13.

Lernhilfen auf Seiten 29, 30

Translate into English. (Übersetze ins Englische.)

a) Wo können wir uns treffen?

_____

b) Wenn du dich verspätest, musst du dich entschuldigen.

_____

_____

c) Tony stellt sich bei seinem neuen Chef vor.

_____

d) Wenn dich das Buch interessiert, kannst du es selbst lesen.

_____

_____

e) Ich kann mich nicht an diesen Lärm gewöhnen.

_____

f) Die Kinder setzen sich und konzentrieren sich auf ihre Arbeit.

_____

_____

g) Jenny fürchtet sich vor dem wilden Hund.

_____

h) Sally and Jane amüsierten sich auf Johns Geburtstagsparty.

_____

_____

i) Peter hat die Königin selbst in London gesehen.

_____

Die reziproken Pronomen

Bill and Joan work in the same office: They see **each other** every day.
Sie sehen sich jeden Tag. ☐

Bill and Joan are good friends: They always help **one another.**
Sie helfen sich immer. ☐

● Das deutsche **sich, sich gegenseitig** oder **einander** wird mit **each other** oder **one another** wiedergegeben, wenn eine **wechselseitige** (= reziproke) **Beziehung** zwischen Personen ausgedrückt werden soll, z. B. jeder sieht den anderen täglich.

Unterschied zwischen

Reflexivpronomen   und   **reziprokem Pronomen**

Tom and Jerry could see **themselves** in the clear water.

Nick and Bob could not see **each other** because of the fog.

Tom und Jerry konnten sich im klaren Wasser sehen. ☐

Nick und Bob konnten sich wegen des Nebels nicht sehen. ☐

● **Reflexiver Gebrauch:** Sie konnten sich selber sehen.

● **Reziproker Gebrauch:** Sie konnten sich nicht sehen (einer den andern).

34

14.
Lernhilfen auf Seite 34

Fill in the correct reflexive or reciprocal pronoun, where necessary.
(Setze das richtige reflexive und reziproke Pronomen, wo es notwendig ist, ein.)

a) Hello. How are you? We haven't seen _____ for quite a time.

b) The girls enjoyed _____ very much at the party.

c) I can't help you, girls. You must do your homework _____.

d) Alan and John always do their homework together.

They help _____.

e) Tina never helps others. She only thinks of _____.

f) Pamela washed _____ and dressed _____ carefully before she went out.

g) Peter and David are good friends. They have known _____ for many years.

h) The five children liked _____ very much.

i) Mary and Tony met _____ at the cinema.

j) Tim has hurt _____ badly with a knife.

k) When Jim was late he had to apologize _____.

l) Sarah knows that we don't like _____.

m) Tony and Sally saw the Queen _____ in London.

n) Help _____ to some more coffee, Clara.

C

15.
Lernhilfen auf Seiten 29 und 34

Translate into English. (Übersetze ins Englische.)

a) Bitte, Nancy, geh und wasch dich.

_____

b) Die Arbeiter machten sich eine Tasse Tee.

_____

c) Mr Walker fühlte sich sehr hungrig.

_____

d) Tony konnte sich an nichts erinnern.

_____

e) Sandra drehte sich plötzlich um und schaute uns an.

_____

f) Die Klingel läutet. Ich gehe selbst und öffne die Tür.

_____

g) Mein Bruder weiß, dass wir uns nicht mögen.

_____

h) Die zwei Mannschaften haben seit drei Jahren nicht gegeneinander gespielt.

_____

_____

i) Kannst du dich an die letzten Ferien erinnern?

_____

j) Der Hund und die Katze hatten voreinander Angst.

_____

k) Der kleine Bill fürchtet sich vor dem Hund.

_____

Adjektiv – Adverb

Der Unterschied im Gebrauch von Adjektiv und Adverb

Wiederholung aus Band 2, Seite 44

16.

Adjective or Adverb? (Adjektiv oder Adverb?)

a) German is a _____ (difficult) language.

b) Ian understands German very _____ (good).

c) He was working _____ (careful) last week.

d) He was able to do all the exercises _____ (easy).

e) His pronunciation will be _____ (excellent) in a few months.

f) If he tries to think in German, he will learn it _____ (fast).

g) He can spell all the words he learns _____ (correct).

h) He remembers _____ (difficult) words _____

_____ (automatic).

i) If you ask Ian something, he doesn't get _____

(nervous) and answers all questions _____ (polite).

j) It's _____ (easy) to listen to

Ian's German because he speaks _____ (clear) and

_____ (slow).

D

● Das Adjektiv nach bestimmten Verben

Mary looks **nice** in her new dress.

Mary sieht in ihrem neuen Kleid nett aus. ☐

This cake tastes very **good.**

Dieser Kuchen schmeckt sehr gut. ☐

● Nach einer bestimmten Gruppe von Verben steht ein **Adjektiv** (und kein Adverb der Art und Weise).

Nach **folgenden Verben,** aber nur in der aufgeführten Bedeutung, steht ein **Adjektiv:**

☐	to become	=	*werden*
☐	to feel	=	*sich fühlen*
☐	to get	=	*werden*
☐	to grow	=	*werden*
☐	to keep	=	*bleiben*
☐	to look	=	*aussehen*
☐	to seem	=	*scheinen*
☐	to smell	=	*riechen*
☐	to sound	=	*klingen*
☐	to stay	=	*bleiben*
☐	to taste	=	*schmecken*

17.

Lernhilfen auf Seite 38

Translate into English. (Übersetze ins Englische.)

a) Die Geschichte dieses Films klingt aufregend.

_____

b) Sarah fühlte sich wunderbar. Sie wurde sehr aufgeregt.

_____

c) Ihr Freund Peter blieb kühl.

_____

d) Das Essen im Restaurant schmeckte köstlich.

_____

e) Der Wein war warm. Er roch schrecklich.

_____

f) Peter wurde sehr ärgerlich.

_____

g) Sarah sah großartig aus. Sie schien nur ein bisschen müde zu sein.

_____

_____

h) Peter und Sarah fühlten sich glücklich.

_____

i) Draußen wird es bald kalt werden.

_____

j) Peters Idee klang nicht schlecht.

_____

k) Sarah sah nicht überrascht aus.

_____

Gleiche Form von Adjektiv und Adverb

Mr Brown has got a **fast** car.	*Herr Brown hat ein schnelles Auto.* ☐
He drives very **fast.**	*Er fährt sehr schnell.* ☐
The train was **early.**	*Der Zug kam (zu) früh.* ☐
Mr Brown gets up **early.**	*Herr Brown steht früh auf.* ☐

● Einige **Adverbien** haben im Englischen die **gleiche Form** wie die entsprechenden **Adjektive.**

Merke:

daily	=	*täglich* ☐	hard	=	*hart, schwer* ☐	
early	=	*früh* ☐	high	=	*hoch* ☐	
enough	=	*genug* ☐	late	=	*spät* ☐	
far	=	*weit* ☐	long	=	*lang* ☐	
fast	=	*schnell* ☐	near	=	*nahe* ☐	

Adverbien mit zwei Formen

Tony works very **hard.**	*Tony arbeitet sehr hart.* ☐
Jonn **hardly** learns anything.	*John lernt kaum etwas.* ☐
Tony doesn't live **near.**	*Tony wohnt nicht in der Nähe.* ☐
It's **nearly** 10 o'clock.	*Es ist fast 10 Uhr.* ☐

● Einige Adverbien haben **zwei Formen** mit **verschiedenen Bedeutungen,** z. B. hard oder hardly.

Merke:

fair	=	*fair* ☐	fairly	=	*ziemlich* ☐	
hard	=	*hart* ☐	hardly	=	*kaum* ☐	
late	=	*spät* ☐	lately	=	*in letzter Zeit* ☐	
near	=	*nahe,* ☐	nearly	=	*fast, beinahe* ☐	
		in der Nähe				

18.

Lernhilfen auf Seite 40

Fill in the right words and use their correct form.
(Setze die richtigen Wörter ein und verwende die korrekte Form.)

a) This was a _____ match. All players were _____

good. The trainer _____ had any problems. His team

will be very successful in the _____ future. All the players

played _____ well because of their _____ training. The plane

was _____ and they arrived home _____ in the evening.

(late 2×, daily, fair 3×, hard, near)

b) Bettina's new horse is _____ and it can jump _____.

Bettina must get up _____ because the stables are

_____ away from her home. She often rides

her horse over _____ distances and sometimes returns

_____.

(fast, fair, high, long, early, far, late)

c) Last month Bettina had a _____ competition and she

_____ won first prize. Her horse ran very

_____ and she had _____ time to watch

the other competitors. She _____ fell off the horse

when she was not careful _____.

(enough 2×, hard, nearly 2×, fast)

D

19. *Lernhilfen auf Seite 40*

Translate into English. (Übersetze ins Englische.)

a) Der 8-Uhr-Zug fährt täglich.

_____

b) Mein Onkel Willi hat ein schnelles Auto, aber er fährt nicht schnell.

_____

_____

c) Es ist spät, Tom. Geh ins Bett. Du musst morgen früh aufstehen.

_____

_____

d) Tom hat kaum Zeit am Wochenende. Er muss fast immer arbeiten. Er arbeitet sehr schwer.

_____

_____

e) Bob ist ein naher Verwandter von uns. Er wohnt nahe bei uns.

_____

_____

f) Der Präsident sprach nicht lange. Es war keine lange Rede.

_____

_____

g) Ian spricht ziemlich fließend Deutsch.

_____

h) Der Mount Everest ist ein hoher Berg. Die Männer kletterten hoch hinauf.

_____

_____

20.

Lernhilfen auf Seiten 37, 38, 40

Adjective or Adverb? Fill in and use the given words.
(Adjektiv oder Adverb?)

a) The Nolans have decorated their rooms. The whole family worked very

_____ and they had a _____ decorator.

So they _____ managed to finish before the weekend.

Today is Saturday and it's a _____ day. The Nolans

want to go to the zoo. Nick and Helen look very _____

because they like travelling by train. It goes so _____.

(happy, beautiful, hard, easy, good, fast)

b) They are a little _____ and so they must walk to the

station _____. Nick buys the tickets and puts them

_____ in his pocket. After a few minutes the

Nolans are sitting in the last carriage and the train starts _____.

Nick feels a little _____ because the ticket inspector

was _____ with him last time. But there is no inspector

today. At the zoo the children want to see the chimps first. They are so

_____.

(angry, careful, late, funny, quick, slow, nervous)

Die Steigerung des Adverbs

Es gibt drei Arten der Steigerung:

hard	hard**er**	hard**est**	☐
fast	fast**er**	fast**est**	☐
high	high**er**	high**est**	☐
early	earl**ier**	earl**iest**	☐

● Steigerung mit **-er/-est**: Adverbien mit der gleichen Form wie die Adjektive.
(Siehe Seite 40)

clearly	**more** clearly	**most** clearly	☐
easily	**more** easily	**most** easily	☐
happily	**more** happily	**most** happily	☐

● Steigerung mit **more/most**: Adverbien auf -ly.

well	**better**	**best**	☐
badly	**worse**	**worst**	☐
much / a lot	**more**	**most**	☐
a little	**less**	**least**	☐

● **Unregelmäßige** Steigerung: Diese Formen musst du auswendig lernen.

a little = wenig

21.

Lernhilfen auf Seite 44

Put the words in brackets in their correct forms.
(Setze die Wörter in Klammern in ihrer richtigen Form ein.)

a) Sarah Simpson sang _____ last night, but Joan

   Sutherland sang even _____. (beautiful)

b) John did the exercise _____, but Judith did

   it even _____. (clever)

c) Tom works _____, but Peter works even _____. (hard)

d) Clara gets up _____ every morning. She gets up _____
   than her brother. (early)

e) Men drive _____ than women, but young people under

   20 drive _____ of all. (careless)

f) Mr Heath has no books. He reads _____.

   He reads even _____ than Mr Hunt. (little)

g) Mr Eaton always dresses _____. He dresses

   _____ than his secretary.

   Mr Huston, their boss dresses _____ of them all. (correct)

h) Barbara plays tennis _____. She plays it _____

   than Judy, but Diane plays _____ in their club. (good)

i) Jack did _____ in his last Latin test, but Nancy did even

   _____ and Mick did _____ of them all. (bad)

45

22.

Lernhilfen auf Seite 44

Translate into English. (Übersetze ins Englische.)

a) Richard ist ein schneller Läufer. Er läuft schneller als seine Klassenkameraden.

_____

_____

b) Charlie Chaplin war ein wunderbarer Schauspieler. Er spielte all seine Rollen hervorragend.

_____

_____

c) Mr Traynor spricht fließend Russisch, aber Deutsch spricht er noch besser.

_____

_____

d) Jack Hunter ist ein ausgezeichneter Schwimmer. Er schwimmt schneller als Tim Cocker, aber Dawn Fraser schwimmt am schnellsten.

_____

_____

e) Mr Jones machte die Übersetzung sehr genau. Er ist ein sehr guter Übersetzer.

_____

_____

f) Gillian isst weniger als ihr Bruder. Ihre Großmutter isst am wenigsten.

_____

_____

Verb: Gegenwart

Present Progressive und Simple Present
Wiederholung aus Band 1 und Band 2

23.

Present Progressive or Simple Present? (Verlaufsform der Gegenwart oder einfache Gegenwart?)

a) You can't talk to Bill at the moment. He _____ (have) a shower.

b) The boys had better not go out. It _____ (begin) to rain.

c) What _____ (you, have) for breakfast, John?

   – I _____ (have) coffee and toast today, but

   I usually _____ (have) tea and cornflakes.

d) What _____ (you, look at)?

   – I _____ (look at) that beautiful car.

e) Can you see that plane over there?

   – Yes, it _____ (just, take off).

f) Our neighbour's dog never _____ (bark) at night.

   It _____ (make) a terrible noise just now.

g) Where _____ (you, go), Jean?

   – I _____ (go) to the cinema.

h) Why _____ (the boys, not do) their homework?

   – Because they _____ (listen, just) to pop music.

Verb: Vergangenheit

● Simple Past und Present Perfect
·Wiederholung aus Band 2, Seite 71

24.
Simple Past or Present Perfect?

a) _____ (you, be, ever) to France?

   – Yes, I _____ (be) there two years ago.

b) My uncle _____ (just, arrive).

   I _____ (not, meet) him for three months.

   I _____ (ring) him twice last week.

   My friend Tom _____ (know) him for three three years.

c) When _____ (you, see) Mr Miller?

   – I _____ (not, see) him, this morning, but

   yesterday I _____ (meet) him at the library.

d) _____ (you, have) breakfast yet?

   – Yes, I _____ (have) breakfast at 8 o'clock.

e) What _____ (you, do) with your shoes? They are dirty.

   – Oh, I _____ (go) out in the rain

   and I _____ (not, clean) them when I

   _____ (come) home.

f) _____ (you, see) Martin the last few days?

   – No, I _____ (not, see) him since Monday.

25.

Translate into English. (Übersetze ins Englische.)

a) Hast du den Brief schon geschrieben? – Ja, ich habe ihn gestern Abend geschrieben.

_____

_____

b) Wann ist dein Zug angekommen? – Er kam heute um zehn Uhr an.

_____

_____

c) Jim hat gestern seinen Geldbeutel verloren und hat ihn noch nicht wieder gefunden.

_____

_____

d) Warst du schon einmal in Irland? – Ja, wir waren dort im letzten Sommer.

_____

_____

e) Wann hast du Paul zum letzten Mal gesehen? – Ich habe ihn seit einem Jahr nicht mehr getroffen.

_____

_____

f) Diana ist schon drei Tage lang krank. Sie hat sich letztes Wochenende erkältet.

_____

_____

Das Present Perfect Progressive

Formen

I	**have been**	work**ing**	*ich habe gearbeitet*	☐
you	**have been**	wait**ing**	*du hast gewartet*	☐
he			*er*	
she	**has been**	play**ing**	*sie* } *hat gespielt*	☐
it			*es*	
we	**have been**	read**ing**	*wir haben gelesen*	☐
you	**have been**	study**ing**	*ihr habt gelernt*	☐
they	**have been**	sleep**ing**	*sie haben geschlafen*	☐

have been / has been + **-ing**

● Du bildest das **Present Perfect Progressive** (= die Verlaufsform des Present Perfect) mit **have been** bzw. **has been** und der **-ing Form** (= Present participle, Partizip Präsens).
● Verneinung: I **have not been working** (= I haven't been working)
● Frage: **Have** you **been waiting?**
● Verneinte Frage: **Have** they **not been playing?**
   (= Haven't they been playing?)

Anwendung

I started working at **8 o'clock.** It is **12 o'clock** now:

I have been working	for 4 hours now.	*Ich arbeite schon seit 4 Stunden.* ☐
I have been working	the whole morning.	*Ich arbeite schon den ganzen Morgen.* ☐
I have been working	since 8 o'clock.	*Ich arbeite schon seit 8 Uhr.* ☐

● Du berichtest mit dem **Present Perfect Progressive** über eine Handlung, die in der **Vergangenheit begonnen** hat (um 8 Uhr früh) und die **noch andauert** oder **gerade beendet** ist (um 12 Uhr).
● Zeitbestimmungen: for (+ now), since (+ now), the whole morning/day/night, all day/night (sinngemäß: bis jetzt).
● Bei der Übersetzung ins Deutsche nimmst du oft das **Präsens** und **schon.**

26.

Lernhilfen auf Seite 50

Use Present Perfect Progressive and 'for' or 'since'.
(Verwende die Verlaufsform des Present Perfect und 'for' oder 'since'.)

a) How long _____ (Tom, wait)?

 – He _____ two hours.

b) How long _____ (your parents,
 live) here?

 – They _____ here _____ 1987.

c) How long _____
 (you and Paul, write) to each other?

 – We _____
 over a year now.

d) How long _____
 (Ian, speak) Russian? ·

 – He _____ Russian _____ 10 years.

e) How long _____
 (your friends, stay) at your house?

 – They _____ with us _____ 3 weeks.

f) How long _____ (it, rain)?

 – It _____ 12 o'clock.

g) How long _____ (these pupils, learn)
 English?

 – They _____ 3 years.

Present Perfect Simple und Present Perfect Progressive

They **have been** here all day.	They **have been working** all day.
How long **have** you **had** this book?	How long **have** you **been waiting?**
We **have known** Tom for a month.	We **have been playing** all day.
She **has wanted** to meet us.	She **has been learning** for an hour.
I **have** always **liked** Barbara.	I **have been waiting** for Barbara.

● Du verwendest das **Present Perfect Simple** vor allem bei folgenden Verben:

be	= *sein*	☐
have	= *haben*	☐
know	= *kennen*	☐
want	= *wollen*	☐
like	= *mögen*	☐
hear	= *hören*	☐
believe	= *glauben*	☐
see	= *sehen*	☐
belong to	= *gehören*	☐

● Du verwendest das **Present Perfect Progressive** vor allem bei Verben, die eine Tätigkeit ausdrücken, und zwar dann, wenn du das **Andauern einer Handlung** betonen willst (z. B. all day). Wenn du dich aber für das Resultat einer Handlung interessierst, verwendest du das **Present Perfect Simple** (z. B. They have worked).

● Bei anderen Verben kannst du es verwenden, wenn dich das **Resultat einer Handlung** interessiert.

● Wiederhole im Band 2, Seiten 66–70.

27.

Lernhilfen auf Seite 52

Complete the dialogue. Use Present Perfect or Present Perfect Progressive.
(Vervollständige den Dialog.)

Mrs Baker and her husband are talking about holidays.

a) Mr Baker: We _____ (not, have) a holiday for the

last five years. Let's go to Blackpool this year. We _____

_____ (never, be) there before.

b) Mrs Baker: Oh, that's wonderful. I _____

(always, want) to go there. Look, I _____
(buy) a new pair of trousers for you.

c) Mr Baker: Oh great. I _____ (look for)
some nice ones for some weeks.

Do you know that we _____ (not, see)
our friends for a long time?

d) Mrs Baker: Yes, that's true. They _____

(live) in Blackpool for three years now, and they _____

_____ (not, be) here since last summer.

What's the title of the book which _____

_____ (you, read) the last few days?

e) Mr Baker: It's 'Holidays in Britain'. I _____
(read) it with great interest.

28. *Lernhilfen auf Seiten 50 und 52*

Translate into English. (Übersetze ins Englische.)

a) Tom und Susan sitzen gerade im Café.

_____

b) Tom: Wie lange wohnt ihr schon in dieser Stadt?

_____

   Susan: Wir wohnen schon seit 1996 hier.

_____

c) Tom: Und wie lange arbeitet dein Vater schon in dieser Fabrik?

_____

   Susan: Er arbeitet dort schon seit zwei Jahren.

_____

d) Tom: Seit wann hast du diesen schönen Ring?

_____

   Susan: Ich habe ihn seit meinem letzten Geburtstag.

_____

e) Tom: Bist du schon einmal in Yorkshire gewesen?

_____

   Susan: Nein, ich bin noch nie dort gewesen. Ich wollte immer schon die Yorkshire Moors besuchen.

_____

_____

f) Tom: Ich lese seit zwei Wochen ein Buch über Nordengland.

_____

_____

Das Past Perfect

Formen

I	**had**	**played**	*ich hatte gespielt*	☐
you	**had**	**taken**	*du hattest genommen*	☐
he	**had**	**come**	*er war gekommen*	☐
she	**had**	**had**	*sie hatte gehabt*	☐
it	**had**	**rained**	*es hatte geregnet*	☐
we	**had**	**been**	*wir waren gewesen*	☐
you	**had**	**seen**	*ihr hattet gesehen*	☐
they	**had**	**arrived**	*sie waren angekommen*	☐

had + **past participle**

- Du bildest das **Past Perfect** (= Plusquamperfekt) mit **had** und dem **past participle** (= Partizip Perfekt).

- Verneinung: **I had not played** (= I hadn't played)
- Frage: **Had it rained?**
- Verneinte Frage: **Had you not seen?** (= Hadn't you seen?)

Anwendung

Barbara told her mother yesterday that she had broken a vase.

Tom was late for school because he had missed the bus.

Mary had finished her homework when her parents came home.

Judy had had breakfast before she went to school.

- Du verwendest das **Past Perfect** zusammen mit dem **Simple Past,** wenn du über Geschehnisse berichtest, die in der **Vergangenheit aufeinander folgten** (z. B. gestern erzählte Barbara, dass sie eine Vase zerbrochen hatte).
- Der Vorgang, der zeitlich **voranging** (z. B. sie hatte die Vase zerbrochen), steht im **Past Perfect,** der andere im **Simple Past** (z. B. sie erzählte davon gestern ihrer Mutter).

55

29.

Lernhilfen auf Seite 55

Fill in the Past Perfect. (Setze das Past Perfect ein.)

a) Tom washed his hands after he _____ (work) in the garden.

b) After I _____ (read) the newspaper I gave it to my father.

c) When the boys arrived, the film _____ (start).

d) Mrs Kenyon cleared the table after the guests _____ (go).

e) As soon as the referee _____ (arrive), the match started.

f) John asked his friend what he _____ (hear) about the accident.

g) After Jeff _____ (score) a goal, the pupils cheered loudly.

h) Paul told his mother that he _____ (get) a bad mark.

i) Pamela watched TV after she _____ (do) her homework.

j) Clara _____ (not, eat) anything before she visited us.

k) The passengers got some drinks after the plane _____ (take off).

l) Billy had to climb through the window because he _____ (forget) his key.

m) My uncle went to Australia as soon as he _____ (finish) school.

n) Tony discovered that someone _____ (steal) his bike.

30.

Lernhilfen auf Seite 55

Make your own sentences. (Bilde eigene Sätze.)

Michael went to visit London last August.

Example (Beispiel):

Saturday: arrived / went to see his friends

After he had arrived, he went to see his friends.

a) Sunday: went to the Tower / visited / Madame Tussaud's

_____

_____

b) Monday: did some shopping in Oxford Street / went to a cinema in Soho

_____

_____

c) Tuesday: visited the Zoo / had a meal at a Chinese restaurant

_____

_____

d) Wednesday: looked at paintings in the National Gallery / listened to an open-air
      concert

_____

_____

e) Thursday: saw the Changing of the Guard / met his girl-friend Susy

_____

f) Friday: paid for his room / took the next train to Dover

_____

31.

Lernhilfen auf Seite 55

Complete the following sentences. Fill in Past Perfect or Simple Past.
(Vervollständige die folgenden Sätze.)

a) How long _____ (Mr Traynor, know) his wife

   before he _____ (marry) her in 1982?

b) He _____ (meet) her in 1977 after they _____

   _____ (live) in the same street for three years.

c) He _____ (tell) her that he _____ (see)

   her before and that he _____ (like) her at once.

d) After Jean _____ (introduce) Ian to her parents,

   they _____ (become) good friends.

e) Before Ian _____ (go) to Russia, he _____ (be)
   to Germany for one year.

f) As soon as Ian _____ (arrive) in Germany,

   he _____ (write) a letter to Jean and _____
   (tell) her to book the next flight to Munich.

g) After Ian _____ (teach) at a school in Munich,

   he _____ (go) to Frankfurt.

h) After the Traynors _____ (stay) in Germany for one year, they

   _____ (return) to Scotland.

i) When Ian _____ (finish) his studies at uni-

   versity, the Traynors _____ (move) to Reading.

Verb: Zukunft

 Going to-Future und will-Future

Wiederholung aus Band 2, Seite 85

32.

Put in the correct form of the 'going to' or 'will-Future'.
(Setze die richtige Form der 'going to' oder 'will-Zukunft' ein.)

The Kenyons are planning a weekend in the Peak District.

a) Mr Kenyon: The weather forecast says that it _____
(be) fine at the weekend.

b) Mrs Kenyon: That's all right, but if it rains, we _____

_____ (not, be able to) go walking.

c) Karen: What _____ (we, do) in Kent Dad?

d) Mr Kenyon: We _____ (have) a picnic, but we

_____ (not, stay) in a hotel

because it's too expensive. I phoned a hostel. We _____

_____ (sleep) there.

e) John: What _____ (we, do) on Saturday?

f) Mr Kenyon: I think on Saturday we _____ (walk)
along that nice little river near Buxton.

g) Karen: Well, but what _____ (we, do) on Sunday?

h) Mrs Kenyon: On Sunday I hope that we _____
(be able to) get as far as Buxton. We can't stay outdoors very

long. It _____ (be) dark at six.

59

● Das Future Progressive

Formen

I	**will** **be**	go**ing**	*ich werde gehen*	☐
you	**will** **be**	spend**ing**	*du wirst verbringen*	☐
he	**will** **be**	com**ing**	*er wird kommen*	☐
she	**will** **be**	ring**ing**	*sie wird anrufen*	☐
it	**will** **be**	rain**ing**	*es wird regnen*	☐
we	**will** **be**	eat**ing**	*wir werden essen*	☐
you	**will** **be**	wait**ing**	*ihr werdet warten*	☐
they	**will** **be**	swimm**ing**	*sie werden schwimmen*	☐

will be	+	-ing

- Du bildest das **Future Progressive** (= Verlaufsform in der Zukunft) mit **will be** und der **-ing Form** des Verbs.
- Kurzformen: **I'll be going, you'll be spending** . . .
- Verneinung: You **will not be** (= You won't be) **spending**
- Frage: **Will** he **be coming?** Where **will** she **be ringing?**
- Verneinte Frage: **Will** you not **be** (= Won't you be) **waiting?**

Anwendung

This time next month we'**ll be flying** to New York.

Come at five. Then Peter **won't be doing** homework.

- Das **Future Progressive** nimmst du für eine Handlung, die zu einem **Zeitpunkt** in der **Zukunft** abläuft.

33.

Lernhilfen auf Seite 60

Peter and his friend have made plans for the weekend. (Peter und sein Freund haben Pläne für das Wochenende gemacht.)
Say what they will be doing. (Sage, was sie tun werden.)

Saturday	
8 o'clock	have a big breakfast together
9 o'clock	get their bikes ready
9.30	set off for a bicycle trip
12.30	have a picnic at a nice lake
for the night	stay at a youth hostel
in the evening	sit together and sing songs
Sunday	
morning	go to church
at noon	return home

Example (Beispiel):

At 8 o'clock they will be having a big breakfast together.

a) _____

b) _____

c) _____

_____

d) _____

_____

e) _____

_____

f) _____

g) _____

34.

Lernhilfen auf Seite 60

Use Future Progressive. (Verwende das Future Progressive.)

a) What _____ (you, do) tomorrow afternoon?

 – I'm sure, I _____ (stay) at home.

b) This time next week we _____ (swim) in the North Sea.

c) We must hurry! Our train _____ (leave) in two minutes.

d) My friend _____ (stay) in America for another year.

e) Fasten your seatbelts. We _____ (land) in a few minutes.

f) You can visit the Kenyons at eleven. They _____

 _____ (not, have) breakfast then.

g) _____ (you, go) to town tomorrow? You could buy some newspapers for me.

h) When you arrive at the Channel it _____ (rain).

i) Tony _____ (do) his homework from 5 to 7.

j) I _____ (write) a letter to my aunt soon.

k) The pupils _____ (study) hard next term.

l) We _____ (wait) for you at the usual time.

m) My friends _____ (swim) in the sea this time next week.

● Das Future Perfect

Formen

I	**will have**	**played**	*ich werde gespielt haben*	☐
you	**will have**	**read**	*du wirst gelesen haben*	☐
he	**will have**	**bought**	*er wird gekauft haben*	☐
she	**will have**	**done**	*sie wird getan haben*	☐
it	**will have**	**arrived**	*es wird angekommen sein*	☐
we	**will have**	**worked**	*wir werden gearbeitet haben*	☐
you	**will have**	**worked**	*ihr werdet gekommen sein*	☐
they	**will have**	**paid**	*sie werden bezahlt haben*	☐

| **will have** | + | **past participle** |

- Du bildest das **Future Perfect** (= zweites Futur) mit **will have** und dem **past participle** (= Partizip Perfekt).
- Verneinung: **I will not have played.** (= I won't have played.)
- Frage: **Will** she **have done** it?
- Verneinte Frage: **Will** we **not have worked?** (= Won't we have worked?)

Anwendung

Clara **will have finished** her homework by 5 o'clock.

Next year Bob **will have been** at this school for 6 years.

- Das **Future Perfect** drückt aus, dass etwas zu einem **bestimmten Zeitpunkt geschehen sein wird** (z. B. by 5 o'clock = bis spätestens 5 Uhr).

G

35.
Lernhilfen auf Seite 63

Use the Future Perfect. (Verwende das Future Perfect.)

a) By that time tomorrow we _____ (pass) our test.

b) You _____ (do) this exercise in 15 minutes.

c) The bus _____ (leave) before we get to the bus-stop.

d) By the end of the month Tony _____ (read) all these books.

e) On 1st July the Traynors _____ (live) in Reading for exactly 6 years.

f) Has the mechanic repaired your car yet?

  – No, but he _____ (repair) it by next Friday.

g) When does the film start? – At seven. I'm afraid it _____

  _____ (start), before we get there.

h) Are you still working Jane? – Yes, but I _____

  _____ (finish) in a few minutes.

i) The Kenyons _____ (travel) round Bavaria by the end of their holidays.

j) The teacher _____ (answer) all questions by the end of the lesson.

k) Next weekend the boys _____ (see) the new film four times.

● Das 'Present Progressive' Future

Are you **going** to Glasgow next week?

– Yes, we **are visiting** our uncle.

● Du verwendest das **Present Progressive** auch, wenn du einen **Plan** oder etwas in der **Zukunft fest vereinbart** hast.

● Meist steht eine Zeitbestimmung dabei (z. B. soon, next week/month, this evening, . . .).

Formen in Band 1, Seite 50

36.

Lernhilfen auf Seite 65

Make sentences. Use the Present Progressive. (Bilde Sätze. Verwende die Verlaufsform im Präsens.)

Example (Beispiel):

they / come / to lunch / next Sunday

They are coming to lunch next Sunday.

a) I / leave / for London / next week

b) Jenny and I / go / to a film / at 7.30

c) you / go / to Leeds / tomorrow / ?

d) Bill / play / tennis / with me / this afternoon

e) the cafe / close / in half an hour

f) my sister / get married / in summer

g) we / not go / to Stockport / next Sunday

h) they / play / Beethoven / tonight

i) John / fly / to Paris / this weekend

37.

Wiederholung der bisher gelernten Zeiten

Fill in the correct tense of the verbs in brackets. (Setze die richtige Zeit der in Klammern angegebenen Verben ein.)

a) At the moment the boys from John's class _____
(spend) a week at a youth hostel in Yorkshire.

b) John _____ (not be) to Yorkshire so far, so he

_____ (enjoy) his stay there very much.

c) Two days ago, they _____ (visit) the Yorkshire Moors.

d) They _____ (cannot walk) too far

because it _____ (be) too dangerous.

e) Yesterday they _____ (take) a trip to Malham Cove where

they _____ (go) rock-climbing.

f) Before they _____ (start) in the morning, their

teacher _____ (tell) them _____ (be)
very careful.

g) It _____ (be) a beautiful day.

h) The sun _____ (shine) and most of the boys

_____ (eat) their lunch at the top of the cliff.

i) Suddenly they _____ (hear) a shout.

j) Nick _____ (lose) his balance and _____

_____ (fall) onto a ledge, but he _____ (not be) injured.

67

k) The boys and their teacher _____ (run) to the spot

from where they _____ (hear) the cry.

l) John _____ (can pull) Nick up.

m) The teacher said: "You _____ (be) lucky, Nick

that you _____ (not be) seriously injured."

n) "I _____ (never feel) so frightened

in my life", Nick _____ (say) after they

_____ (save) him.

o) What _____ the boys _____ (do) tomorrow?

p) They all hope that the weather _____ (not be)

too bad. Then they _____ (can go) swimming
in one of the beautiful lakes.

q) Perhaps some of them _____ (hire) a rowing-

boat, others _____ (just lie) in the sun.

r) By the end of the week the boys _____ (see)
a lot of beautiful sights.

s) John _____ (be) sure that he _____
(come) back to Yorkshire some day.

Verb: Andere Formen

● Das Passiv

Simple Present

I	**am**	**asked**	*ich werde gefragt*	☐
you	**are**	**invited**	*du wirst eingeladen*	☐
he she it	**is**	**taken**	*er sie es* wird genommen	☐
we	**are**	**brought**	*wir werden gebracht*	☐
you	**are**	**sent**	*ihr werdet geschickt*	☐
they	**are**	**held**	*sie werden gehalten*	☐

am
is + **past participle**
are

● Du bildest das **Passiv** (= the passive) im **Simple Present** mit einer Form von **to be** (am, is, are) und dem **past participle** (= Partizip Perfekt, 3. Form des Verbs).

Passivsätze mit 'by'

The police stop the driver.	*Die Polizei hält den Fahrer an.*	☐
The driver **is stopped** by the police.	*Der Fahrer wird von der Polizei angehalten.*	☐
They repair the car in the garage.	*Sie reparieren das Auto in der Werkstatt*	☐
The car **is repaired** in the garage.	*Das Auto wird in der Werkstatt repariert.*	☐

● Wenn du ausdrücken willst, **wer** eine Handlung ausführt, schließt du den **Urheber** (z. B. Polizei) mit **by** . . . an. Dies gilt für alle Zeiten.

38. *Lernhilfen auf Seite 69*

Use the passive in the Simple Present. (Verwende das Passiv in der einfachen Gegenwart.)

a) to plant Potatoes _____ in spring.

b) to repair Cars _____ at a garage.

c) to check The tyre pressure _____ by the mechanic.

d) to sell All kinds of things _____ at the supermarket.

e) to wear Bathing-suits _____ in summer.

f) to pick Apples and pears _____ not _____ in spring.

g) to keep Milk _____ in the fridge.

h) to drive Taxis _____ by taxi-drivers.

i) to put on Pyjamas _____ at night.

j) to play Football _____ all over the world.

k) to visit The Tower _____ by many people.

l) to build A lot of roads _____ in our country.

m) to speak English _____ in many countries.

n) to watch Television _____ in most homes.

o) to read Newspapers _____ every day.

● Das Passiv

Modale Hilfsverben

The letter	**must**	**be**	**written.**	*Der Brief muss geschrieben werden.* ☐
The address	**can**	**be**	**changed**	*Die Adresse kann geändert werden.* ☐
The museum	**may**	**be**	**entered.**	*Das Museum darf betreten werden.* ☐
The car	**should**	**be**	**washed.**	*Das Auto sollte gewaschen werden.* ☐
The bike	**ought to be**		**repaired.**	*Das Fahrrad sollte repariert werden.* ☐
The seat	**has to**	**be**	**cleaned.**	*Der Sitz muss gereinigt werden.* ☐

| modal | + | be | + | past participle |

● Du kannst das **Passiv** (= the passive) auch mit **modalen Hilfsverben** (= modals) oder deren **Ersatzformen** und **be** und dem **past participle** bilden.

● Wenn es nötig ist, kannst du den Urheber der Handlung mit **by** anfügen, z. B. The museum may be entered **by everybody.**

71

H

39.

Lernhilfen auf Seite 71

Use the passive. (Verwende das Passiv.)

Farmer Jackson is a busy man:
He has to feed the animals early in the morning.
He must milk the cows before seven o'clock.
He ought to cut the grass before lunch.
He has to repair a plough after lunch.
He could clean the tractor after lunch.
First he should repair a fence in the afternoon.
He must plough a field before it gets dark.
He has to plant potatoes before 7 p.m.
He can dig the garden in the evening.

One morning he thinks of all the work he has to do during the day.

Example (Beispiel):

The animals have to be fed early in the morning.

a) The cows _____ before seven o'clock.

b) The grass _____

c) _____

d) _____

e) _____

f) _____

_____

g) _____

h) _____

● Das Passiv

Simple Past

I	**was**	**served**	*ich wurde bedient*	☐
you	**were**	**left**	*du wurdest verlassen*	☐
he she it	**was**	**run over**	*er sie wurde überfahren es*	☐
we	**were**	**understood**	*wir wurden verstanden*	☐
you	**were**	**stopped**	*ihr wurdet angehalten*	☐
they	**were**	**found**	*sie wurden gefunden*	☐

was
were + **past participle**

● Du bildest das **Passiv** (= the passive) im **Simple Past** mit einer Form von **to be** (was, were) und dem **past participle**.

73

40.

Lernhilfen auf Seite 73

What happened to Mr Carey? (Was passierte Herrn Carey?)

Use the following verbs. (Verwende die folgenden Verben.)

> visit – knock down – call – bandage – interview – take 2× – send – question
> carry – operate – put

a) Last week Mr Carey _____ by a car.

b) An ambulance _____ .

c) Mr Carey _____ to the nearest hospital.

d) He _____ upstairs.

e) There he _____ on a bed in the First Aid room.

f) His leg _____ on by a doctor.

g) It _____ by a nurse.

h) Then he _____ to a single room.

i) The next day he _____ by his wife.

j) Three days later he _____ by newspaper reporters.

k) After a week he _____ by the police.

l) Four weeks later he _____ home.

● Das Passiv

will-Future

	will	be	served	*ich werde bedient werden*	☐
you	will	be	chosen	*du wirst gewählt werden*	☐
he she it	will	be	seen	*er sie es wird gesehen werden*	☐
we	will	be	asked	*wir werden gefragt werden*	☐
you	will	be	called	*ihr werdet gerufen werden*	☐
they	will	be	opened	*sie werden geöffnet werden*	☐

will be	+	past participle

● Im **will-Future** bildest du das **Passiv** (= the passive) mit **will be** und dem **past participle**.

75

41.

Lernhilfen auf Seite 75

What will be done tomorrow? (Was wird morgen getan werden?)

the garage doors	steal
the flowers	smash
the windows	do
Tom's bike	cook
questions	open
dinner	repair
all my money	play
the exercises	ask
the camera	clean
the match	water
a new supermarket	paint

The garage doors will be painted.

a) _____

b) _____

c) _____

d) _____

e) _____

f) _____

g) _____

h) _____

i) _____

j) _____

● Das Passiv

Present Perfect

I	**have been**	**carried**	*ich bin getragen worden*	☐
you	**have been**	**pushed**	*du bist gestoßen worden*	☐
he she it	**has been**	**seen**	*er sie ist gesehen worden es*	☐
we	**have been**	**called**	*wir sind gerufen worden*	☐
you	**have been**	**beaten**	*ihr seid geschlagen worden*	☐
they	**have been**	**bought**	*sie sind gekauft worden*	☐

have been
has been   +   **past participle**

● Du bildest das **Passiv** (= the passive) im **Present Perfect** mit **have/has been** und dem **past participle.**

42.

Say what has happened. (Sage, was sich ereignet hat.)

Use the following elements. (Verwende die folgenden Teile.)

A lot of work	repair / at the garage
My father's car	do / today
A million pounds	not find / yet
This room	steal / from the bank
Tony	run over / by a lorry
Barbara's bike	not allowed / in schools
The Browns' cat	clean / this week
The windows	not invite / to our party
Smoking	break / by the boys

Example (Beispiel):

A lot of work has been done today.

a) _____

b) _____

c) _____

d) _____

e) _____

f) _____

g) _____

h) _____

● Das Passiv

Past Perfect				
I	had been	driven	*ich war gefahren worden*	☐
you	had been	asked	*du warst gefragt worden*	☐
he she it	had been	found	*er sie es war gefunden worden*	☐
we	had been	left	*wir waren verlassen worden*	☐
you	had been	chosen	*ihr wart gewählt worden*	☐
they	had been	closed	*sie waren geschlossen worden*	☐

had been + **past participle**

● Im **Past Perfect** bildest du das **Passiv** (= the passive) mit **had been** und dem **past participle.**

79

H

43.

Lernhilfen auf Seite 79

Put into Past Perfect. (Setze ins Past Perfect.)

a) The bike was stolen.

_____

b) The air was let out of the tyre.

_____

c) The door is damaged.

_____

d) Some beer bottles were dropped on the floor.

_____

e) The tickets have been sold.

_____

f) England was conquered by the Romans.

_____

g) The roads are blocked.

_____

h) The football match has been postponed.

_____

i) The Spanish Armada was defeated by the English.

_____

j) Two pedestrians were injured.

_____

k) A new president will be chosen.

_____

● Das Passiv

Present Progressive

I	**am**	**being**	**asked**	*ich werde (gerade) gefragt*	☐
you	**are**	**being**	**pushed**	*du wirst (gerade) gestoßen*	☐
he she it	**is**	**being**	**tested**	*er sie es wird (gerade) geprüft*	☐
we	**are**	**being**	**visited**	*wir werden (gerade) besucht*	☐
you	**are**	**being**	**called**	*ihr werdet (gerade) gerufen*	☐
they	**are**	**being**	**tested**	*sie werden (gerade) geprüft*	☐

$$\boxed{\begin{array}{c}\textbf{am}\\\textbf{are}\\\textbf{is}\end{array}} + \boxed{\textbf{being}} + \boxed{\textbf{past participle}}$$

● Du bildest das **Present Progressive** (= die Verlaufsform im Präsens) im **Passiv** mit **am / are / is** + **being** + dem **past participle.**

Past Progressive

I	**was**	**being**	**served**	*ich wurde (gerade) bedient*	☐
you	**were**	**being**	**chosen**	*du wurdest (gerade) gewählt*	☐
he she it	**was**	**being**	**taken**	*er sie es wurde (gerade) gebracht*	☐
we	**were**	**being**	**interviewed**	*wir wurden (gerade) interviewt*	☐
you	**were**	**being**	**noticed**	*ihr wurdet (gerade) bemerkt*	☐
they	**were**	**being**	**repaired**	*sie wurden (gerade) repariert*	☐

$$\boxed{\begin{array}{c}\textbf{was}\\\textbf{were}\end{array}} + \boxed{\textbf{being}} + \boxed{\textbf{past participle}}$$

● Das **Past Progressive** (= Verlaufsform im Past) bildest du im **Passiv** mit **was / were** + **being** und dem **past participle.**
● Im Passiv gibt es die Verlaufsform nur im Present Tense und Past Tense.

44.   *Lernhilfen auf Seite 81*

Translate into English. (Übersetze ins Englische.)

a) Die Straße wird (gerade) repariert.

_____

b) Du wirst (gerade) gerufen.

_____

c) Ich wurde (gerade) bedient.

_____

d) Die Brücken wurden (gerade) gebaut.

_____

e) Alan wird (gerade) geprüft.

_____

f) Der Minister wurde (gerade) interviewt.

_____

g) Das Treffen wurde (gerade) abgehalten.

_____

h) Der Patient wird (gerade) operiert.

_____

i) Wir wurden (gerade) gefragt.

_____

j) Die Motoren werden (gerade) verbessert.

_____

k) Diese Häuser waren (gerade) im Bau.

_____

45. *Lernhilfen auf Seiten 69, 71, 73, 75, 77, 79*
Put into active or passive. (Setze ins Aktiv oder Passiv.)

a) Do they check all suitcases?

_____

b) Somebody can open our suitcases.

_____

c) Last time my bag wasn't opened.

_____

d) An officer has just found a pistol.

_____

e) That man will be searched carefully.

_____

f) Is his passport taken away by an officer?

_____

g) They can send him to prison, can't they?

_____

h) If the pistol had not been found, the man might have killed other people.

_____

_____

i) Did anyone find the diamonds?

_____

j) These men unload the plane and fill up the tanks.

_____

_____

46.

Lernhilfen auf Seiten 69, 71, 73, 75, 77, 79, 81

Translate into English. (Übersetze ins Englische.)

a) Wenn ein Flugzeug gelandet ist, wird es entladen.

_____

b) Wird das Gepäck gewogen werden?

_____

   – Ja. Nachdem das Gepäck gewogen worden ist, muss es zum Flugzeug gebracht und eingeladen werden.

_____

_____

c) Wenn Stichproben gemacht werden, müssen die Passagiere ihre Ausweise vorzeigen.

_____

_____

d) Zwanzig Flaschen Wein mussten verzollt werden.

_____

e) Letztes Mal wurde Herr Müller nicht durchsucht.

_____

f) Nachdem das Gepäck durchsucht worden war, wurde es zur Halle gebracht.

_____

_____

g) Eines der Flugzeuge wird gerade von einigen Arbeitern entladen.

_____

_____

Die -ing Form (Gerund)

nach bestimmten Verben

Bob's uncle enjoyed smoking.   *Bobs Onkel rauchte gern.*   ☐

He gave it up and started eating sweets.   *Er gab es auf und fing an*
                                           Süßigkeiten zu essen   ☐

● Nach bestimmten Verben (z. B. **enjoy**) steht das folgende Verb in der **-ing Form**
  (= Gerund).

Verben + -ing Form

to avoid	= *vermeiden*	☐	to love	= *lieben*	☐
to dislike	= *nicht mögen*	☐	to mind	= *etwas dagegen*	
to enjoy	= *genießen*	☐		*haben*	☐
to finish	= *beenden*	☐	to prefer	= *vorziehen*	☐
to hate	= *hassen*	☐	to start	= *anfangen*	☐
to like	= *mögen, gern tun*	☐	to suggest	= *vorschlagen*	☐
			to stop	= *aufhören*	☐

* Bei diesen Verben ist auch der Infinitiv möglich, z. B.: He started to eat sweets.

47. *Lernhilfen auf Seite 85*

Choose a gerund and finish the sentences. (Wähle ein Gerund aus und vervollständige die Sätze.)

> being – driving – walking – telling – buying – dancing – going – opening –
> laughing – going – smoking – flying – taking – eating

a) Johnny hates _____ told that he was late for school.

b) Would you mind _____ the window? It's too hot in here.

c) Timothy loves _____ his car fast.

d) Judy enjoyed _____ at Peter's party.

e) Mr Miller couldn't help _____ when he heard the story.

f) Billy prefers _____ to _____ by car, but his girlfriend

   Jenny suggests _____ their bikes.

g) Charles is an honest boy. He avoids _____ lies.

h) Mary, I feel like _____ to the cinema. Are you coming
   with me?

i) My uncle stopped _____ so many cigarettes.

   He started _____ sweets instead.

j) The Prestons can't avoid _____ a new car. Their old one
   cannot be repaired.

k) Why don't you fly to England? – I dislike _____ in a plane.

● Die -ing Form (Gerund)

nach Verb + Präposition

Bob's uncle gave up smoking.

Bobs Onkel gab das Rauchen auf. ☐

He is thinking of doing
more sports.

*Er denkt daran, mehr Sport zu
treiben.* ☐

He thanked her for helping him.

*Er dankte ihr dafür, dass sie ihm
geholfen hatte.* ☐

● Nach bestimmten **Verben,** die mit einer **Präposition** verbunden sind, z. B. give
+ up, think + of, thank + for, folgt die **-ing Form** des Verbs.

● Im Deutschen musst du dir eine **freiere Übersetzung** überlegen.

Verben mit Präposition

to dream of	= *träumen von*	☐
to give up	= *aufgeben*	☐
to look forward to	= *sich freuen auf*	☐
to talk about	= *darüber sprechen*	☐
to thank for	= *dafür danken*	☐
to think of	= *daran denken*	☐

48.

Lernhilfen auf Seite 87

Find a preposition and complete the sentences by using the -ing form. (Finde eine Präposition und vervollständige die Sätze mit der -ing Form.)

a) Let's go _____ _____ (do) the next exercise.

b) You shouldn't give _____ _____ (try) because it's not difficult.

c) You parents will thank you _____ _____ (work) so hard.

d) Perhaps you can also talk with your friend _____ _____ (help) you.

e) If you are thinking _____ _____ (do) your extra work at the weekend, this will be all right.

f) Have you never dreamt _____ _____ (become) the best pupil in your class?

g) When you have found the right solutions you can quietly look forward _____

_____ (write) your next test.

● Die -ing Form (Gerund)

nach Adjektiv + Präposition

Tony is interested in reading books about South America.

Tony ist daran interessiert, Bücher über Südamerika zu lesen. ☐

He is keen on visiting these countries one day.

Er ist darauf aus, diese Länder eines Tages zu besuchen. ☐

He is fond of speaking Spanish.

Er spricht sehr gerne Spanisch. ☐

● Du verwendest die **-ing Form** auch nach **Adjektiven**, die mit einer **Präposition** verbunden sind, z. B. **interested + in, keen + on.**

Adjektive mit Präpositionen

to be afraid of	= *Angst haben vor*	☐
to be ashamed of	= *sich schämen vor*	☐
to be fond of	= *sehr gern mögen*	☐
to be good at	= *gut . . . können*	☐
to be interested in	= *interessiert sein an*	☐
to be keen on	= *darauf aus sein*	☐
to be proud of	= *stolz sein auf*	☐
to be tired of	= *einer Sache leid sein*	☐

49. *Lernhilfen auf Seite 89*

Rewrite the sentences using a gerund. (Schreibe die Sätze noch einmal und verwende ein Gerund.)

Example (Beispiel):

Barbara goes to the cinema. (keen on)

Barbara is keen on going to the cinema.

a) Paul won the swimming contest last Saturday. (proud of)

_____

b) Angela plays the piano. (good at)

_____

c) Pamela likes to ride horses. (fond of)

_____

d) David doesn't want to go out when it's dark. (afraid of)

_____

e) Stanley likes to read books about the Antarctic. (interested in)

_____

_____

f) Barbara's mother doesn't always want to have to tell her to tidy her room. (tired of)

_____

_____

g) Georgie made some mistakes in his last test. (ashamed of)

_____

_____

● Die -ing Form (Gerund)

nach Substantiv + Präposition

Mr Carter had no opportunity of
learning German.

Herr Carter hatte keine Gelegen-
heit Deutsch zu lernen. ☐

● Die **-ing Form** steht auch nach **Substantiven**, die mit einer **Präposition**
verbunden sind, z. B. **opportunity + of.**

Substantive mit Präpositionen

chance of   = *Möglichkeit* ☐
in danger of   = *in Gefahr* ☐
opportunity of   = *Gelegenheit* ☐

nach Präpositionen

After arriving at the station, I noticed
that the train had left.

Nachdem ich am Bahnhof
angekommen war, bemerkte ich,
dass der Zug abgefahren war. ☐

● Du verwendest die **-ing Form** nach einer **Präposition*.**
● Im Deutschen entspricht der Konstruktion **Präposition + Gerund** in der Regel
ein **Nebensatz**, z. B.: Nachdem ich am Bahnhof angekommen war.

Präpositionen*

after   = *nachdem* ☐
before   = *bevor* ☐
instead of = *anstatt* ☐

50.

Lernhilfen auf Seite 91

Link the two sentences. (Verbinde die beiden Sätze.)

Example (Beispiel):

Hans will travel to Scotland. He has the opportunity.

Hans has the opportunity of travelling to Scotland.

a) Hans learns English at school. He has the chance.

_____

_____

b) Hans will live in Scotland for a year. He has the opportunity.

_____

c) Mr Brown will lose his money. He is in danger.

_____

d) Hans doesn't fly to Scotland. He goes by ferry. (instead of)

_____

e) He had found the cheapest way. Then he booked his ticket. (after)

_____

f) He told Helga about his plans. Then he invited her for a coffee. (before)

_____

_____

g) He said good-bye to all his friends. Then he left. (after)

_____

51.

Lernhilfen auf Seiten 85, 87, 89

Translate into German. (Übersetze ins Deutsche.)

a) Liz: Have you ever thought of leaving your country?

_____

b) Don: Yes, I'd be interested in seeing foreign countries.

_____

c) Liz: Can you imagine living in another country for many years?

_____

_____

d) Don: Well, I wouldn't be keen on living abroad for years.

_____

_____

e) Liz: But couldn't you think of going for a shorter time?

_____

f) Don: Yes. After passing my exams, I'd be keen on seeing parts of South America.

_____

_____

g) Liz: Maybe you would enjoy working there.

_____

h) Don: Yes. I'm dreaming of getting a good job. So I wouldn't mind spending some time there.

_____

_____

Der Infinitiv nach Fragewörtern

Bob showed me	how	**to draw.**	*Bob zeigte mir, wie ich das Bild zeichnen sollte.* ☐
I didn't know	where	**to start.**	*Ich wusste nicht, wo ich anfangen sollte.* ☐
I had no idea	who	**to ask.**	*Ich hatte keine Ahnung, wen ich fragen sollte.* ☐

- Nach Fragewörtern (z. B. how, where, who) kannst du den **Infinitiv mit to** verwenden.
- Diese Konstruktion ist kürzer als ein Nebensatz mit einem modalen Hilfsverb, z. B.: I didn't know where I should start.
  - → I didn't know where to start.

Der Infinitiv nach Adjektiven

It's	expensive	**to go**	by car. *Es ist teuer, mit dem Auto zu fahren.* ☐
It's	more expensive	**to fly.**	*Es ist teurer zu fliegen.* ☐
It's	most expensive	**to go**	by taxi. *Es ist am teuersten, mit dem Taxi zu fahren.* ☐
It's	cheapest	**to go**	by bike. *Es ist am billigsten, mit dem Fahrrad zu fahren.* ☐

- Nach Adjektiven in der Grundform und in den Steigerungsstufen (Komparativ und Superlativ) kann der **Infinitiv mit to** stehen.

52.

Lernhilfen auf Seite 94

Rewrite the sentences. (Schreibe die Sätze neu.)

Example (Beispiel).

The boys don't know where they should put their bikes.

The boys don't know where to put their bikes.

a) They don't know how they can get to Reading.

_____

b) The girls always know who they might ask.

_____

c) They told the boys when they could catch a train.

_____

d) But David and Jean didn't remember what they should bring with them.

_____

e) They wondered how they could get from the station to their uncle's.

_____

f) They easily found out where they could meet.

_____

g) Jean wondered who she could ask for information.

_____

h) She asked a conductor: "Can you tell me where I can buy my ticket?"

_____

i) In the end they could not decide which train they should take.

_____

53.

Lernhilfen auf Seite 94

Find a question word and finish the sentences. (Finde ein Fragewort und vervollständige die Sätze.)

a) Can you explain to me _____ (get) to Soho?

b) The policeman showed the old lady _____ (cross) the street.

c) The girls couldn't decide _____ (go) to the cinema. At six or at eight.

d) Can you tell me _____ (pronounce) the word 'Worcester'?

e) The children must find out _____ (get up) in the morning.

f) Mr Potter doesn't understand _____ (use) a computer.

g) Mrs Baker can't decide _____ (wear) in the evening.

h) Mr Traynor has been wondering _____ (buy) good wine.

i) His wife told him _____ (bake) a cake.

j) The boys don't know _____ (ask) for the way.

k) Billy showed his little sister _____ (ride) a bike.

l) Georgie discovered _____ (get) cheap sweets.

m) John didn't remember _____ (do) first.

54.

Lernhilfen auf Seite 94

Translate into German. (Übersetze ins Deutsche.)

a) Clara isn't sure what to wear at Jill's party.

_____

b) The boy scouts found out how to cross the river.

_____

c) The children had no idea what to do at the weekend.

_____

d) My friend told me when to meet him at the station.

_____

e) John doesn't know who to ask for help.

_____

f) He hesitates about which bus to take.

_____

g) Margaret wondered where to buy some stamps.

_____

h) Could you tell me how to get to the Town Hall?

_____

i) Mr Smith was told when to start work.

_____

j) When Mr Clark arrived he didn't know where to hang his coat.

_____

_____

55.

Lernhilfen auf Seite 94

Rewrite the sentences. (Schreibe die Sätze neu.)

Example (Beispiel):

Tony will be glad <u>when he gets</u> the letter.

Tony will be glad to get the letter.

a) Bob was happy <u>when he heard</u> that he had passed his exam.

b) Columbus was the first man <u>who discovered</u> America.

c) Can you tell me the best pub <u>where I can have lunch?</u>

d) George is always the last <u>who arrives</u> in the morning.

e) Clara will be the next pupil <u>who will be examined.</u>

f) Mr Brown was sorry <u>when he read about</u> the accident.

g) Mr Jones was the oldest man <u>who took part in</u> the marathon.

h) We were surprised <u>when we saw</u> our friends again.

i) Nick is too lazy. <u>He doesn't help</u> his father.

● Objekt + Infinitiv mit to

Tom wanted **his sister to join** the club.

Tom wollte, dass seine Schwester dem Club beitrat. ☐

I would like **you to post** the letter.

Ich möchte, dass du den Brief einwirfst. ☐

● Nach **want** und **would like** können **Objekt** und der **Infinitiv mit to** stehen.

● Beachte die deutsche Übersetzung: . . ., **dass** . . .

TIP	Im Englischen darfst du, im Gegensatz zum Deutschen, keinen Objektsatz mit **that** bilden.

Falsch: ~~Tom wanted that his sister joined~~ the club.

56.

Lernhilfen auf Seite 99

Translate into English. (Übersetze ins Englische.)

a) Tom wollte nicht, dass sein Bruder wegläuft.

_____

b) Er wollte, dass er zu Hause bleibt.

_____

c) Ich will, dass du die Tür schließt.

_____

d) Warum willst du, dass ich die ganze Arbeit allein tun muss?

_____

_____

e) Mrs Kenyon möchte gern, dass John seinen Onkel besucht.

_____

_____

f) Möchtest du, dass Jean dich am Sonntag anruft?

_____

g) Die Kinder wollen, dass ihnen Großmutter eine Geschichte erzählt.

_____

_____

h) Frau Johnson möchte, dass ihr Sohn die Tochter ihrer Freundin heiratet.

_____

_____

Modale Hilfsverben

● Can – Must – May
Wiederholung aus Band 1, Seiten 62, 64, und Band 2, Seiten 89, 90, 93, 95

57.
Translate into English. (Übersetze ins Englische.)

a) Peter hat nicht kommen können.

_____

b) Wird Jane antworten können?

_____

c) Ian musste gestern zu Hause bleiben.

_____

d) Alan wird morgen früh aufstehen müssen.

_____

e) Tony durfte seine Freunde nicht besuchen.

_____

f) Frau Miller brauchte nicht lange zu warten.

_____

g) Werden wir am Wochenende arbeiten müssen?

_____

h) Bill hatte uns nicht anrufen können.

_____

i) Herr Brown hat sein Auto verkaufen müssen.

_____

● Can – Could

Can I borrow your pen, please?
Kann ich bitte deinen Füller ausleihen? ☐

Could you tell me the way to the station, please?
Könnten Sie mir bitte den Weg zum Bahnhof sagen? ☐

● **Could** heißt **könnte.** Es ist etwas höflicher als **can.**

Paul **could** understand the Irishman.
Paul konnte den Iren verstehen. ☐

Mary **couldn't** catch the bird.
Mary konnte den Vogel nicht fangen. ☐

● **Could** heißt hier **konnte.** Es drückt eine Fähigkeit aus. Du verwendest es vor allem bei Verben wie **understand, see, hear.** Bei anderen Verben nimmst du **was able to / were able to.**

● **Couldn't** heißt **konnte nicht.** Es drückt eine Unfähigkeit aus. Du kannst es anstelle von **was not able to / were not able to** bei allen Verben verwenden.

58.

Lernhilfen auf Seite 102

Finish the sentences. (Vervollständige die Sätze.)

Use could / couldn't, was / were able to. (Setze ein.)

> think properly – buy a camera – see the match – play tennis – post the letter
> – hear the birds – open the door

a) Peter got some pocket money, so he _____.

b) Sandra didn't have a racket, so she _____.

c) Mr Penn had no key, so he _____.

d) Jane had some stamps, so she _____.

e) Bill turned down the radio, so he _____.

f) Georgie climbed a tree, so he _____.

> walk far – show films – run the marathon – think properly – check his maths
> homework – understand the announcer – jump over the wall

g) Clara was tired, so she _____.

h) The girls didn't feel well, so they _____.

i) Tom trained very hard, so he _____.

j) Bob had a calculator, so he _____.

k) The youth leader had a video recorder, so he _____.

l) The horse was old, so it _____.

m) The boys listened attentively, so they _____.

● May – Might

Tom isn't at home:

He **may be** in London.

He **may have gone** by bus.

Tom ist nicht zu Hause:

Er ist vielleicht in London. ☐

Er ist vielleicht mit dem Bus gefahren. ☐

● **May** drückt eine **Möglichkeit** oder **Vermutung** aus. Im Deutschen entspricht dies oft **vielleicht.**

● **May + Perfektkonstruktion,** z. B. **may have gone,** drückt aus, dass etwas **möglicherweise** oder **sehr wahrscheinlich** geschehen ist.

Tom hasn't returned. It's late:

He **might** still **be** in London.

He **might have missed** the last bus.

Tom ist noch nicht zurück-gekehrt. Es ist spät.

Er könnte vielleicht noch in London sein. ☐

Er könnte möglicherweise den letzten Bus versäumt haben. ☐

● **Might** drückt eine **Vermutung** aus, die ziemlich **unsicher** oder **unwahrschein-lich** ist. Im Deutschen entspricht dies oft **könnte vielleicht** oder **könnte möglicherweise.**

● **Might + Perfektkonstruktion,** z. B. **might have missed,** drückt aus, dass etwas **möglicherweise** geschehen sein **könnte.**

104

59.

Lernhilfen auf Seite 104

Fill in might, mightn't or might have. (Setze ein.)

a) If Tom and Judy are in Wales they _____ go on a bicycle tour.

b) Going too long distances _____ be a good idea.

c) Jerry and Anne _____ come with them if Tom had asked them.

d) Judy was afraid that her bike _____ be good enough.

e) She took a coat with her because she thought it _____ rain.

f) Tom is angry that Judy is so late. She _____ telephoned.

g) Judy said: "You _____ believe it, Tom, but I couldn't find my key."

h) Tom _____ be right, but Judy doesn't think he is.

i) Judy and Tom wondered why their friends hadn't come.

   They _____ missed the train.

j) Tom said: "You must phone them, Judy. They _____ still be at home."

k) Paul _____ lend you his bike, but I'm not sure if he will.

l) It _____ be a good idea to walk all the way, but let's try.

60.

Lernhilfen auf Seite 104

Translate into German. Try to find the difference between may and might.
(Übersetze ins Deutsche. Versuche den Unterschied von may und might wiederzugeben.)

a) Do the football pools, Peter. You may win a few pounds.

_____

_____

b) Ring Barbara up first. She might not be at home. She might have gone to Liverpool.

_____

_____

c) The Millers are not at home tonight. They may have gone to the cinema.

_____

_____

d) Peter's team are angry because they lost the match. They might have won if they had played more effectively.

_____

_____

e) If Susy looks after the baby, the parents may go for a long walk.

_____

_____

f) We don't know yet what to do this afternoon, but we might go to the youth club.

_____

_____

● Will – Would

| **Will** | *Teilweise Wiederholung aus Band 2, Seite 83* |

Peter **will** visit his aunt next year. | *Peter wird nächstes Jahr seine Tante besuchen.* ☐

She **will** show him Glasgow if she has time. | *Sie wird ihm Glasgow zeigen, wenn sie Zeit hat.* ☐

● Mit **will** bildest du die **Zukunft** (= will-Future).
● Du nimmst das **will-Future** auch im **Bedingungssatz: Typ 1.** (Seite 112)

Would

I	**would**	go	*ich würde gehen*	☐
you	**would**	ask	*du würdest fragen*	☐
he she it	**would**	come	*er sie es* } *würde kommen*	☐
we	**would**	eat	*wir würden essen*	☐
you	**would**	answer	*ihr würdet antworten*	☐
they	**would**	read	*sie würden lesen*	☐

would + **Infinitiv**

● Mit **would** und dem **Infinitiv** bildest du das **Konditional** (= Conditional). Du nimmst es auch im **Bedingungssatz: Typ 2** (Seite 115) und in **der indirekten Rede** (Seite 133).

I	**would have**	gone	*ich wäre gegangen*	☐
you	**would have**	asked	*du hättest gefragt*	☐
he she it	**would have**	come	*er sie es* } *wäre gekommen*	☐
we	**would have**	eaten	*wir hätten gegessen*	☐
you	**would have**	answered	*ihr hättet geantwortet*	☐
they	**would have**	read	*sie hätten gelesen*	☐

would have + **past participle**

● **Would have** + **past participle** verwendest du auch im **Bedingungssatz: Typ 3** (Seite 118) und in **der indirekten Rede**.

107

61.

Translate into English. (Übersetze ins Englische.)

a) Ich würde die Polizei anrufen.

_____

b) Jenny würde nicht im Regen spazieren gehen.

_____

c) Ein gebrauchtes Fahrrad wäre nicht so teuer wie ein neues.

_____

d) Ein Taxi wäre sehr teuer gewesen.

_____

e) Die Mädchen hätten die Zeitung gelesen.

_____

f) Würdet ihr uns am Wochenende besuchen?

_____

g) Nick und Bill werden ihren Onkel nächste Woche fragen.

_____

h) Sie werden nicht mit dem Zug fahren.

_____

i) Hätten sie den Fahrplan gelesen?

_____

j) Sie würden den nächsten Bus nehmen.

_____

k) Ihr Onkel hätte es ihnen gesagt.

_____

l) Ihre Tante wäre zu Hause.

_____

● Should – Ought to

It's cold outside.   *Es ist kalt draußen.*

You **should** / **ought to** } wear a cap.   *Du solltest eine Mütze aufziehen.* ☐

● **Should** und **ought to** entsprechen dem Deutschen **sollte** (eigentlich / lieber / besser).

● Verneinung: You **shouldn't/oughtn't to** do that.

● Frage: **Should** I go? **Ought** I **to** go?

Tom **should** / **ought to** } have asked   *Tom hätte fragen sollen.* ☐

● **Should** und **ought to** + **Perfektkonstruktion** (z. B. should have asked / ought to have asked) drücken aus, dass etwas **hätte geschehen** oder **getan werden sollen**.

109

62. *Lernhilfen auf Seite 109*
'Ought to' or 'oughtn't to' or 'ought to have'? (Setze ein.)

a) The music on the radio is too loud.

Ian _____ turn it down.

b) Cigarettes are bad for your health, Bill.

You _____ smoke them.

c) Tony has got bad marks in English. His father is angry.

Tony _____ learn more.

d) Too much TV isn't good for you, Mary.

You _____ watch all evening.

e) Clara's room is in a big mess.

She _____ tidy it before Mother comes home.

f) Louise has got a temperature.

She _____ stay in bed.

She _____ go to school before Monday.

g) The new film about Australia is very interesting.

You _____ seen it. It's a pity you missed it.

h) I know you've got a lot of homework to do, Jean.

_____ you _____ work longer?

i) The Bronsons missed the last ferry to the Continent.

They _____ taken an earlier train.

j) This is a dangerous crossing.

Something _____ be done by the authorities.

k) Petra is giving a party next Saturday.

_____ we _____ bring some sandwiches?

63.

Translate into German. (Übersetze ins Deutsche.)

a) Billy shouldn't believe every word his friend says.

_____

b) You're old enough, Sandra. You should know better.

_____

c) Should we have checked the tyres before we started?

_____

d) You oughtn't to disturb your father when he is sleeping.

_____

e) Everyone ought to stop when the traffic lights are red.

_____

f) People ought to watch the traffic carefully all the time.

_____

_____

g) Accidents like these shouldn't happen again.

_____

h) Motorists oughtn't to drink alcohol before driving.

_____

_____

i) Jane ought to have practised harder.

_____

Satzgefüge

● Bedingungssätze (= If-Sätze): Typ 1

If I **go** to the disco tonight,	I **will meet** lots of nice people.
If we **don't work** hard,	we **won't get** good marks.

If-Satz: **Present**	Hauptsatz: **will + Infinitiv** (**= will-Future**)

- **If** heißt im Deutschen **wenn, falls.**
- Der **if-Satz** (= if-clause) kann vor oder nach dem Hauptsatz stehen:
  If I go to the disco tonight, I will meet lots of nice people.
  I will meet lots of nice people **if I go to the disco tonight.**
- Im **if-Satz Typ 1** drückst du aus, dass in **Zukunft** (tonight) etwas geschehen wird, wenn eine bestimmte Bedingung (If I go . . .) erfüllt wird.

If I **am** at home this afternoon,	I **can read** my new book.
If I **have** lots of homework to do,	I **needn't help** my father.

If-Satz: **Present**	Hauptsatz: **can** **needn't** **must** } **+ Infinitiv** **might**

- Du kannst im Hauptsatz anstatt **will** ein anderes **modales Hilfsverb** nehmen.

64.
Lernhilfen auf Seite 112

Form sentences with the given parts. (Bilde Sätze mit den vorgegebenen Teilen.)

Example (Beispiel):

it / cold / tomorrow / the girls / go / skiing

If it's cold tomorrow, the girls will go skiing.

a) it / rainy / the boys / not / can / go skating

_____

b) Clara / forget / her umbrella / get / soaked / to the skin

_____

c) Peter / have / enough money / buy / a new bike

_____

d) Betty / be / at home / this afternoon / help / her mother

_____

e) you / eat / too / many sweets / spoil / your teeth

_____

f) Jane / be / in London / before noon / she / not miss / the procession

_____

_____

g) the dog / bark / the baby / cannot sleep

_____

h) Mrs Potter / pay the bill / in time / not have / any trouble

_____

i) Mr Sleeve / not post / the letter / in time / not arrive / before Monday

_____

_____

65.

Lernhilfen auf Seite 112

What will you do if . . .?
Find the right answer. (Finde die richtige Antwort.)

What will you do if it starts to rain?
What will yo do if the weather is fine?
What will you do if you lose your way in London?
What will you do if you miss your bus?
What will you do if your tooth hurts?
What will you do if you win £ 5000?
What will you do if you see a thief coming out of a house?
What will you do if you have got a headache?

- open my umbrella   - go to the dentist's
- wait for the next one   - take a tablet
- go for a long walk   - ask a policeman
- call the police   - give a big party

Example (Beispiel):

If it starts to rain, I'll open my umbrella.

a) _____

b) _____

c) _____

d) _____

e) _____

_____

f) _____

g) _____

Bedingungssätze (= If-Sätze): Typ 2

If I **was** at home now,   I **would read** the newspaper.

If Bob **missed** the train,   he **would take** a bus.

If Jane **had** the money,   she **would buy** a new bike.

If-Satz: **Past**

Hauptsatz: **would + Infinitiv** (= **Conditional**)

● Im **if-Satz Typ 2** drückst du aus, dass etwas geschehen oder sein **könnte,** wenn eine bestimmte Bedingung (If I was . . .) erfüllt würde.

If I **was** at home now,   I **could watch** TV.

If Tom **failed** the exam,   he **might repeat** it.

If-Satz: **Past**

Hauptsatz: **could** **might** } **+ Infinitiv**

● Du kannst beim **if-Satz Typ 2** im Hauptsatz anstatt **would + Infinitiv** auch ein anderes **modales Hilfsverb** (z. B could, might) **+ Infinitiv** verwenden.

115

66.

Lernhilfen auf Seite 115

Put the verbs in brackets into the correct tense. (Setze die Verben in Klammern in die richtige Zeit.)

a) If Janet had enough money, she _____ (buy) a new recorder.

b) We could go swimming if the weather _____ (be) warmer this afternoon.

c) John _____ (not make) so many mistakes if he worked more regularly.

d) Anne might become ill if she _____ (not wear) her warm coat.

e) What would you do if the schoolbus _____ (break down) in the morning?

f) If John won a large sum of money in the lottery, he _____ (spend) his holidays in the USA.

g) I _____ (not drink) that wine if I was you.

h) If Mr Walker _____ (understand) German better, he could telephone his friends in Berlin.

i) Mrs Morell wouldn't get so fat if she _____ (eat) less.

j) I'm sure your friend would help you with your homework if you _____ (ask) him.

k) Where _____ (you, go shopping) if you visited London?

l) Mr Jones _____ (get) a job if he had any qualifications.

m) If I _____ (know) the answers to these questions, I would tell you.

116

67. *Lernhilfen auf Seite 115*

Put the following sentences into type 2. (Setze die folgenden Sätze in Typ 2.)

a) If Mother leaves now, she will get to town on time.

_____

b) If she goes by train, she will arrive earlier.

_____

c) If Ian comes to the party, Jean will come too.

_____

d) If he brings his guitar, Ian will be able to sing country songs.

_____

e) If Jean comes in time, she can help her friend.

_____

f) If you meet her before, you may ask her to bring some records.

_____

g) If Jean's father is at home, he will give her a lift.

_____

h) If everyone comes, Susan will have to make more food.

_____

i) If the weather is fine, the party will take place in the garden.

_____

j) If the bus doesn't arrive on time, they can take a train.

_____

k) If everybody helps a little, it will be a wonderful party.

_____

l) If Jean catches the last bus, she will be home at half past eleven.

_____

Bedingungssätze (= If-Sätze): Typ 3

If I **had been** at home last night,   I **would have finished** my homework.

If Bob **hadn't missed** the train,   he **would have come** on time.

If Jane **had gone** to the party,   she **would have met** her friends.

If-Satz: **Past Perfect**	Hauptsatz: **would have + past participle** (= **Conditional Perfect**)

● Im **if-Satz Typ 3** drückst du aus, dass etwas in der **Vergangenheit** (last night) geschehen oder hätte sein können, wenn eine bestimmte Bedingung (If I had been at home . . .) erfüllt worden wäre.

If I **had been** at home last night,   I **could have phoned** you.

If Ian **had got** a ticket,   he **might have gone** to the theatre.

If-Satz: **Past Perfect**	Hauptsatz: **could have** ⎫ + **past** **might have** ⎭ **participle**

● Du kannst im Hauptsatz anstatt **would have + past participle** auch ein anderes **modales Hilfsverb** (z. B. could have) + **past participle** verwenden.

Du lernst in diesem Jahr die 3 grundlegenden Typen von if-Sätzen. Weitere Kombinationen mit anderem Sinn (z. B. Übung 71, Satz g) folgen später.

68.

Lernhilfen auf Seite 118

Find the answers to the following questions. (Finde Antworten zu den folgenden Fragen.)

Example (Beispiel):

What would you have done if it had been raining? (take/umbrella)

If it had been raining, I would have taken an umbrella.

a) Who could Peter have met if he had been in town? (his girl-friend)

_____

_____

b) What might the boys have done if the weather had been fine? (go on a tour)

_____

_____

c) What would have happened if your father had given up smoking earlier? (not become ill)

_____

_____

d) What would Paul have done if he had known that Janet was coming? (invite / to the cinema)

_____

_____

e) What could Mathew have done if Martha had brought him the books? (read/at the weekend)

_____

_____

69.

Lernhilfen auf Seite 118

Rewrite these sentences. Use an if-clause. (Schreibe die Sätze neu. Verwende einen Bedingungssatz.)

Example (Beispiel):

Bob didn't give Mary the flowers, so she was sad.

If Bob had given Mary the flowers, she wouldn't have been sad.

a) Nicole didn't visit the Tower because she hadn't time.

_____

_____

b) The old man didn't see the car, so he was run over.

_____

_____

c) The driver was injured because he didn't fasten his safety belt.

_____

_____

d) His son didn't know he was in hospital, so he didn't visit him.

_____

_____

e) The driver had an accident because he wasn't careful enough.

_____

_____

f) He was driving very fast. That's why the accident was so bad.

_____

_____

70.

Lernhilfen auf Seiten 112, 115, 118

Finish the following sentences. (Vervollständige die folgenden Sätze.)

a) Mr Parker _____ (buy) a new car if he had the money.

b) If he _____ (not/buy) an old one, he would not have had any trouble.

c) If Paul passes his driving test, he _____ (be allowed to) use his father's car.

d) If his father _____ (offer) him to use the car, he would drive to school.

e) If Mr Parker _____ (be) in a hurry tomorrow, he _____

_____ (not/go) by bus.

f) Mrs Parker _____ (take) the car if it

_____ (be) in the garage yesterday.

g) Paul and his sister _____ (be) glad if their mother gives them a lift.

h) If school _____ (be) out at noon, they can meet in town.

i) If Mr Parker works overtime, he _____ (need/not/work) on Friday.

j) He would be very happy if he _____ (have) a free weekend.

k) He _____ (might/earn) more money last

month if he _____ (work) longer in the evenings.

l) He _____ (go) on a fishing holiday next summer

if his family _____ (come) with him.

71.

Lernhilfen auf Seiten 112, 115, 118

Translate into English. (Übersetze ins Englische.)

a) Was würdest du tun, wenn du viel Geld hättest?

_____

_____

b) Wenn du in der Lotterie gespielt hättest, hättest du vielleicht 10 000 Mark gewinnen können.

_____

_____

c) Wenn dein Vater dir das Geld gäbe, könntest du dir ein neues Rad kaufen.

_____

_____

d) Wenn ich ihn frage, bin ich sicher, dass er mir seins gibt.

_____

_____

e) Tom hätte dir helfen können, wenn er gewollt hätte.

_____

f) Wenn wir nächsten Sommer Ferien in Schottland machen, können wir die Highlands besuchen.

_____

_____

g) Mary würde sicher mit uns kommen, wenn sie nicht letztes Jahr dort gewesen wäre.

_____

_____

● Relativsätze

| who – that |

The boy **who opened the door** was my brother.

This is the girl **who sang.**

The shop **that sells cassettes** is over there.

Peter is wearing trousers **that are too long for him.**

- ● **who opened the door, who sang, that sells cassettes** und **that are too long for him** sind **Relativsätze.**
- ● Das Relativpronomen (z. B. who, that) steht nach einem Substantiv (z. B. boy, shop). Vor diesen Relativsätzen steht **kein Komma.**
- ● **Who** bezieht sich auf **Personen** (deutsch: der, die, das).
- ● **That** bezieht sich auf **Sachen** (deutsch: der, die, das).
- ● In diesen Sätzen sind **who** und **that** Subjekt. (Wer öffnete die Tür? Was ist zu lang?)

| whose |

Jane is the girl **whose mother works at the cafeteria.**

Her father works at a garage **whose owner we know.**

- ● Um die Zugehörigkeit oder den Besitz (wessen?) auszudrücken, verwendest du **whose** (deutsch: dessen, deren).
- ● **Whose** bezieht sich gewöhnlich auf **Personen** (z. B. girl) und **Tiere;** du kannst es jedoch auch bei Sachen (z. B. garage) nehmen.

123

72.

Lernhilfen auf Seite 123

Fill in 'who' or 'that'. (Setze 'who' oder 'that' ein.)

a) The boy _____ lost his book is waiting outside.

b) Is this the car _____ your uncle bought last week?

c) The books _____ you lent me were interesting.

d) The pupil _____ won the prize was only fifteen.

e) Bob Harris was one of the sportsmen _____ won an Olympic medal.

f) My boy-friend _____ lives in London sent me a photo of the Tower.

g) Do you know anyone _____ has got a sailing-boat?

h) Tom enjoyed the film _____ he saw last night.

i) Is there anything in the room _____ is made of wood?

j) Have you seen that man _____ wears a blue coat?

k) My uncle Bill _____ lives in New York has got a big house there.

l) A foreigner is a person _____ comes from or is in another country.

m) A saw is a tool _____ is used for cutting through wood or metal.

n) A pistol is a weapon _____ is fired by one hand.

o) An astronaut is someone _____ is trained for spaceflights.

p) Can you show me the dress _____ you bought in London?

q) Settlers are people _____ colonize a piece of land.

r) A fox is an animal _____ has red fur and a bushy tail.

73.
Lernhilfen auf Seite 123

Make one sentence out of two. (Mache aus zwei Sätzen einen.)

Example (Beispiel):

There's the train. It goes to London.

There's the train that goes to London.

a) The park is on your right. It is Hyde Park.

_____

b) We listened to the guide. He explained everything.

_____

c) This is the Tower. It was a prison in former days.

_____

d) We are in a big street now. It is called Fleet Street.

_____

e) On that column stands Admiral Nelson. He was the hero of Trafalgar.

_____

_____

f) That building is Buckingham Palace. You can see it over there.

_____

_____

g) The flag is flying on the roof. It is the Union Jack.

_____

h) We've seen all the sights. I showed them to you on the map.

_____

_____

74.

Lernhilfen auf Seite 123

Connect the sentences. (Verbinde die Sätze.)

Example (Beispiel):

We saw some lions. Their cage was small.

We saw some lions whose cage was small.

a) We saw some elephants. Their ears were large.

_____

b) There were a lot of monkeys. Their faces were ugly.

_____

c) We saw some birds. Their feathers were blue and red.

_____

d) We saw some girls. Their dresses were pretty.

_____

e) There were some giraffes. Their necks were long.

_____

f) We saw some ponies. Their little ones were tiny.

_____

g) There were some tigers. Their skin was yellow.

_____

h) We saw some fish. Their teeth were terrible.

_____

i) There were some children. Their mothers were angry.

_____

● Relativsätze

Contact clauses

Ian is the man who we met in London.
Ian is the man **we met in London.**

The man who we met in London comes from Scotland.
The man **we met in London** comes from Scotland.

What colour was the blouse that you were wearing yesterday?
What colour was the blouse **you were wearing yesterday?**

The work that we must do is quite interesting.
The work **we must do** is quite interesting.

- ● Hier sind **who** und **that Objekt** des Relativsatzes (Wen trafen wir? Was hast du getragen?).
- ● Wenn **who** und **that** Objekt des Relativsatzes sind, können sie **wegfallen.**
- ● Die Sätze ohne Relativpronomen nennt man **contact clauses.**

Relativsätze mit nachgestellter Präposition

Jenny is the girl who I played with.
Jenny is the girl **I played with.**

Where is the disco that the children go to?
Where is the disco **the children go to?**

- ● Die **Präposition** (z. B. with, to) steht gewöhnlich **am Satzende nach** einem Verb. Dies gilt für Relativsätze mit **who** und **that** oder solchen **ohne** Relativpronomen.

127

75.

Lernhilfen auf Seite 127

Choose the correct answer. (Wähle die richtige Antwort aus.)

a) The book _____ is not on the shelf.
   that I need it – I need – who I need – I need it

b) I enjoyed the book _____.
   who you lent me – that lent me – you lent it me – that you lent me

c) The pupil _____ can have it back.
   whose book I still have – who book I still have – that book I still have

d) The doctor _____ told him he was very ill.
   who he went – to who he went to – he went to – that he went

e) The boy _____ is waiting outside.
   that his lost book – lost his book – who lost his book

f) The girls _____ are coming next weekend.
   who you met here – you met them here – that you met them here

g) The film _____ is the best I've ever seen.
   that I'm thinking – I'm thinking of – of that I'm thinking

h) The car _____ was quite expensive.
   who my uncle drives – whose my uncle drives – that my uncle drives

i) The pupil _____ was only fifteen.
   won the prize – who won the prize – he won the prize

j) This is my boyfriend _____ at the party.
   you met – you met him – who you met him – whose you met

k) A hairdresser is a person _____
   cuts your hair – that your hair cuts – whose cuts your hair – who cuts
   your hair

76.

Lernhilfen auf Seite 127

Translate into German. (Übersetze ins Deutsche.)

a) There's a girl in Helga's class whose father is English.

_____

_____

b) Is it the girl we met in town last Saturday?

_____

c) Yes, and she is the girl whose brother is my boyfriend.

_____

d) The house they live in is the biggest in town.

_____

e) The girl whose name is Heidi often visits her grandparents who live in Brighton.

_____

_____

f) Her grandma is not the kind of lady who would not swim in the sea.

_____

_____

g) Last summer she saved the little girl whose parents are her neighbours.

_____

_____

h) It was the most exciting adventure Heidi had ever had.

_____

_____

77.

Lernhilfen auf Seite 127

Translate into English. (Übersetze ins Englische.)

a) Der Doktor, den Heidis Großmutter anrief, war ein Freund der Familie.

_____

_____

b) Die Nachbarn, deren Auto kaputt war, konnten das Kind nicht holen.

_____

_____

c) Ist dies das Haus, in dem deine Großeltern leben?

_____

d) Wo ist deine Familie, die in diesem Haus lebte?

_____

e) Heidis Großmutter ist eine Frau, die alles besser weiß.

_____

_____

f) Peter hat mir das Buch gezeigt, das er gekauft hat.

_____

g) Es ist das Buch, dessen Geschichte ich kenne.

_____

h) Das Buch, das Peter gekauft hat, ist das schönste, das ich gelesen habe.

_____

_____

● Die indirekte Rede

Grundmuster: Aussage

Tony: "Ian lives in England."

Tony says (that) Ian lives in England.

Tony: "I can't find my book."

Tony tells us that he can't find his book.

● Über eine **Aussage** berichtest du mit **say, tell someone, answer.**
● **That** kann entfallen.

● Je nach Sinn der Aussage musst du das **Personalpronomen** (z. B. I) bzw. das **Possesivpronomen** (z. B. my) verändern.
● Die Zeit des Verbs bleibt gleich, weil die einleitenden Verben im **Present** stehen (says, tells us).

Grundmuster: Frage

Was beachtest du **zusätzlich** bei **indirekten Fragen?**

Sue: "Where is my book?"

Sue wants to know where her book is.

Sue: "Was Peter at home?"

Sue wonders if Peter was at home.

Jack: "Do you play tennis, Bill?"

Jack asks Bill if he plays tennis.

● Du beginnst mit **want to know, wonder, 'd like to know oder ask.**
● Du übernimmst das **Fragewort** der direkten Frage (z. B. where).

● Bei indirekten Yes-/No-Fragen nimmst du **if** oder **whether** (deutsch: ob).

● Die Wortstellung ist wie bei der indirekten Aussage, also:
  He plays tennis
  if he plays tennis.

TIP

Vermeide den häufigen Fehler:
Jack asks Bill if he ~~does play~~ tennis.

131

78.

Lernhilfen auf Seite 131

Change into reported speech. (Wandle in die indirekte Rede um.)

Example (Beispiel):

Alan says: "My girlfriend was late."

Alan says (that) his girlfriend was late.

a) Bob says: "I'm trying to finish the exercise."

_____

b) David asks: "Are we meeting in the evening?"

_____

c) Clare says: "I've been learning hard since September."

_____

d) Pamela says: "I'll work four months for my exam."

_____

e) She adds: "My friend Bob helps me."

_____

f) George wants to know: "Does Jack want to join us?"

_____

g) Clare says: "Our teacher is going to give us some books for our preparation."

_____

_____

h) Pamela says: "I've not told my father about it yet."

_____

i) George says: "I needn't hurry because I've got a lot of time."

_____

● Die indirekte Rede

Einleitendes Verb im Past

Tony: "Bob helps me."

Tony said (that) Bob **helped** him.   helps   →   helped   ☐

Jane: "I'm waiting in the hall."

Jane told us (that) she **was waiting** in the hall.   am   →   was   ☐

Tony: "Are you going to play tennis?"

Tony asked if we **were going to** play tennis.   are   →   were   ☐

The girls: "We have lost our keys."

The girls said (that) they **had lost** their keys.   have   →   had   ☐

● Wenn das **einleitende Verb im Past** steht (z. B.: said, told someone, asked),
so wird das Verb oder das erste Wort eines zusammengesetzten Verbs im
Aussage- und Fragesatz vom **Present** zum **Past** verändert.

Tony: "My friends were late."

Tony said (that) his friends **were** late.   were   =   were   ☐
He said his friends **had been** late.   oder: →   had been

Jane: "I was waiting."

Jane said (that) she **was waiting**.   was   =   was   ☐
She said she **had been waiting**.   oder: →   had been

● Wenn das Verb oder das erste Wort eines zusammengesetzten Verbs im **Past**
steht, kann **Past bleiben** oder es verändert sich zum **Past Perfect**.

133

79.
Lernhilfen auf Seite 133

Put into reported speech. (Setze in die indirekte Rede.)

a) Charles said, "I've got the job and I'm very happy about it."

_____

_____

b) He said, "I was awfully sad that I was out of work."

_____

c) Billy remarked, "My uncle also works in the factory."

_____

d) He said, "I've always wanted to hear something about your job."

_____

_____

e) Sheila said, "I'm playing the guitar at our party."

_____

f) She remarked, "I'm going to ask my brother to give me a lift."

_____

g) Anne declared, "We tell all our friends to go to the concert."

_____

_____

h) Claire pointed out, "I've never heard such lovely music."

_____

_____

80.

Lernhilfen auf Seite 133

Change the following questions into reported speech. (Verwandle die folgenden Fragen in die indirekte Rede.)

a) "Why does Mrs Kenyon like to go to Germany?" Nicole asked.

_____

b) Jill wondered, "How long has she been planning her holidays?"

_____

c) "Is it possible for us all to go on a tour?" the children wanted to know.

_____

_____

d) "When are we going to leave from Dover?" Mr Kenyon asked.

_____

e) "Did you get the tickets?" he asked his wife.

_____

f) "Why haven't you booked a flight?" Maureen asked.

_____

g) "Where can we stay for the first night?" Billy wanted to know.

_____

h) "Who has seen our big suitcase?" said mother.

_____

i) "How long does it take us to get to Calais?" Billy asked.

_____

j) "Do you think you can buy two bags?" Mrs Kenyon asked her husband.

_____

_____

K

● Die indirekte Rede

Tony: "I'll wait for you."

Tony said (that) he **would** wait for me.   will   →   would   ☐

Jane: "Paul may park in the garage."

Jane said (that) Paul **might** park in the garage. may   →   might   ☐

Joe: "I must try hard."

Joe said (that) he **had to** try hard.   must   →   had to   ☐

The boys: "We needn't hurry."

The boys said (that) **they didn't have to** hurry. needn't →   didn't have to   ☐

Bill: "Can we meet at five?"

Bill asked if they **could** meet at five.   can   →   could   ☐

● Die **Modalverben** (= modals) verändern sich ebenfalls.

Tony: "I should get up earlier."

Tony said (that) he **should** get up earlier.   should   =   should   ☐

Jane: "We could wait."

Jane said (that) they **could** wait.   could   =   could   ☐

● **Should, could, might** und **ought to** bleiben **unverändert.**

┌─────────────────────────────┐
│ **Weitere Veränderungen**   │
└─────────────────────────────┘

this → that   here → there
tomorrow → the following day   yesterday → the day before
next month → the following month   last week → the week before
ago → before

81.

Lernhilfen auf Seite 136

Put into reported speech. (Setze in die indirekte Rede.)

a) Tony said, "I started school nine years ago."

_____

b) Paul remarked, "Lizzie won a prize yesterday."

_____

c) Robert added, "We'll win our match tomorrow."

_____

d) Charles pointed out, "I must train harder because I'm not fast enough."

_____

_____

e) Fred shouted, "We needn't be afraid because the others aren't too strong."

_____

_____

f) Charles promised, "We can support you next Saturday."

_____

_____

g) Bob said, "We may learn a lot because we'll get a very good coach."

_____

_____

h) Charles remarked, "We should try to get some more money."

_____

i) Frank pointed out, "We could solve this problem. This is exactly what our coach says."

_____

_____

82. *Lernhilfen auf Seiten 131, 133, 136*

Put the questions into reported speech. (Setze die Fragen in die indirekte Rede.)

a) Will we be meeting our friends when we stay in Munich?" Maureen asked.

_____

_____

b) Mother asked Billy, "Have you been learning enough German at school?"

_____

_____

c) The customs officer asked them, "Have you anything to declare?"

_____

_____

d) Shouldn't we phone the travel agents?" Mr Kenyon asked.

_____

_____

e) "What sort of train can we catch?" the children asked.

_____

f) "Must we change trains at Cologne?" Mr Kenyon wanted to know.

_____

g) Mrs Kenyon's friend asked, "How long will your holidays last?"

_____

h) "Will you be back at the end of August?" she asked her.

_____

i) "Who are your friends you will visit in Germany?" she wanted to know.

_____

_____

83. *Lernhilfen auf Seiten 131, 133, 136*

Translation: Write down the dialogue in direct speech. (Übersetzung: Schreibe den Dialog in direkter Rede.)

a) *Der Arzt fragt, was dir fehlt.*

   Doc.: "_____?"

b) *Du erzählst ihm, dass du seit Monaten Husten hast und ihn nicht loswirst.*

   You: " _____"

   _____

c) *Er will wissen, ob du starker Raucher bist.*

   Doc.: "_____?"

d) *Du bejahst dies und sagst dann, dass du gewöhnlich fünf bis zehn Zigaretten am Tag rauchst, gelegentlich aber auch fünfzehn.*

   You: " _____

   _____"

e) *Er fragt, ob dir klar ist, dass Rauchen äußerst ungesund ist.*

   Doc.: "_____?"

f) *Du erwiderst, dass dir das egal sei, weil du ja noch jung bist.*

   You: " _____"

g) *Er will wissen, ob du jemals versucht hast, das Rauchen aufzugeben.*

   Doc.: "_____?"

h) *Du erzählst ihm, dass du es schon zweimal versucht hast, dass du es aber nicht geschafft hast.*

   You: "Well, _____"

   Doc.: "I can help you there."

Fragesätze

 Fragebildung in allen Zeiten

Wiederholung aus Band 1, Seiten 6, 72, 75, 80, und Band 2, Seiten 102, 103

Frage-wort	Hilfsverb Ersatz-hilfsverb	Subjekt	Verb	andere Wörter
	Does	Ian	read	a lot?
	Did	Joan	watch	television?
	Will	Iris	visit	Germany?
	Has	Bob	come	in time?
	Would	Jill	ask	her father?
Where	have	you	had	this letter?
When	did	Bob	finish	the course?
How long	have	the Millers	been living	in this town?
Why	is	Jean	going to stay	in Austria?
		Who	answered	the question?
		What	happens	at school?
		Which of you	has been	to London?
		Whose car	came	first?

● Yes/No-Fragen beginnen mit einem Hilfsverb (z. B. **Will, Has**) oder Ersatzhilfs-verb (z. B. **Does, Did**), andere Fragen mit einem Fragewort (z. B. **Where, When**).

● Wird nach dem Subjekt gefragt (z. B. **Who**), dann ist die Wortstellung: **Fragewort** (= Subjekt) **– Verb – andere Wörter.**

84.

Lernhilfen auf Seite 140

Ask for the underlined parts. (Frage nach den unterstrichenen Teilen.)

a) Maureen and Bob went <u>to Scotland</u> on holiday.

_____

b) They travelled by train <u>because they thought it was the cheapest way to spend their holidays.</u>

_____

c) Bob bought <u>a pair of shoes and a rucksack</u> before they started.

_____

d) They set off <u>on the first Monday in August.</u>

_____

e) It took them <u>four hours</u> to get to Carlisle.

_____

f) Near Loch Lomond they met <u>an old Scotsman.</u>

_____

g) He asked them <u>to spend a few days in his house.</u>

_____

h) After three days <u>Maureen and Bob</u> said 'good bye' to the old man.

_____

i) They stayed in the Highlands for <u>two</u> weeks.

_____

j) They found <u>a nice little inn</u> on their way to Aberdeen.

_____

k) Bob and Maureen returned from their trip <u>after twenty days.</u>

_____

141

● Fragebildung mit nachgestellten Präpositionen

Who does the book belong **to**?	*Wem gehört das Buch?*	☐
What are you looking **for**?	*Was suchst du?*	☐
Where does Ian come **from**?	*Woher kommt Ian?*	☐

● Wird das Fragewort (z. B. who, what, where) durch eine **Präposition** (z. B. to, for, from) näher bestimmt, so tritt sie normalerweise ans **Ende** des Fragesatzes.

85.
Lernhilfen auf Seite 142
Ask for the underlined parts. (Frage nach den unterstrichenen Satzteilen.)

a) Mr Traynor comes from <u>Glasgow</u>.

_____

b) Uncle Henry was talking about <u>his home town</u>.

_____

c) A lot of people are waiting for <u>the bus</u>.

_____

d) Cheese is made from <u>milk</u>.

_____

e) Anne was looking for <u>her English book</u> all the time.

_____

f) Mr Brown was eating with <u>a friend</u> in a Chinese restaurant.

_____

g) The postman has brought a parcel from <u>my grandparents</u>.

_____

h) Bob is very much interested in <u>studying biology</u>.

_____

i) All the mountains are covered with <u>snow</u>.

_____

j) Mrs Traynor sent a Christmas card to <u>her friends</u> in Austria.

_____

k) Maureen and Kate go to <u>a comprehensive</u> school in Reading.

_____

86.

Lernhilfen auf Seite 142

Translate into English. (Übersetze ins Englische.)

a) Von wem hast du den Brief bekommen?

_____

b) Wem gehört dieser Regenschirm?

_____

c) Wovor hat Susy Angst?

_____

d) Weißt du, wonach John suchte?

_____

e) Mit wem haben die Millers letztes Jahr ihren Urlaub verbracht?

_____

_____

f) Für wen hat Mutter ein schönes Geburtstagsgeschenk gekauft?

_____

_____

g) Womit kann Bob seine Schuhe sauber machen?

_____

h) Über wen haben die Leute gestern gesprochen?

_____

i) Wem gehört dieses große Auto dort?

_____

j) Wonach suchen die Kinder?

_____

Wortstellung

● Satzbau: Die Grundmuster
Wiederholung aus Band 1, Seite 87, und Band 2, Seiten 114, 116

87.
Form sentences.

a) their next holiday / in England / the Müllers / will spend

_____

_____

b) are going to / in Cheshire / they / on a canal / a boat / hire

_____

_____

c) a boat / easy / fairly / to steer / is / it

_____

d) already / booked / Herr Müller / in Chester / has / a boat

_____

_____

e) the start / are / the children / waiting for / impatiently

_____

_____

f) go to / a drink / in the evenings / they / for / can / a pub

_____

_____

● Verben mit zwei Objekten

Ian	sent	Jean	a telegram.
Subjekt	**Verb**	**indirektes Objekt**	**direktes Objekt**

- Nach **gewissen Verben** (z. B. send) können **zwei Objekte** stehen, ein **indirektes** (z. B. Jean) und ein **direktes** (z. B. a telegram).
- In diesem Fall drückst du aus, dass Ian ein **Telegramm** (und keinen Brief) schickte.

Ian	sent	a telegram	to Jean.
Subjekt	**Verb**	**direktes Objekt**	**indirektes Objekt**

- In diesem Fall aber willst du das **indirekte Objekt** besonders **hervorheben**: Ian schickte **Jean** (und nicht Jill) ein Telegramm. Du stellst es mit **to** ans Ende des Satzes.

Verben mit zwei Objekten:

to bring	= *bringen*	☐
to give	= *geben, schenken*	☐
to offer	= *anbieten*	☐
to pass	= *reichen*	☐
to sell	= *verkaufen*	☐
to send	= *schicken*	☐
to show	= *zeigen*	☐
to teach	= *lehren*	☐
to tell	= *erzählen, sagen*	☐
to write	= *schreiben*	☐

88.

Lernhilfen auf Seite 146

Answer the following questions. (Beantworte die folgenden Fragen.)

Example (Beispiel):

What did Tom's father give him for Christmas? (a bike)

Tom's father gave him a bike for Christmas.

a) What did Bob send his girlfriend last week? (a letter)

b) Who did Betty write a postcard to? (her grandparents)

c) What does the postman bring Mr Brown? (a parcel)

d) What did grandma tell the children? (a story)

e) Who did Tom show his camera to? (Clara, not Betty)

f) What did Mr Miller sell to the car dealer? (his old car)

g) What did Ian send Jean? (a telegram)

h) What did Mrs Smith pass her husband? (the salt)

i) Who did the manager offer a ticket to? (his friends, not everyone)

M◀

89.

Translate into English. (Übersetze ins Englische.)

Lernhilfen auf Seite 146

a) Peter gab Betty das <u>Buch</u>, nicht das Heft.

_____

b) Betty schrieb <u>Max</u> den Brief, nicht seiner Schwester.

_____

c) Tony zeigte Jean seine <u>Briefmarken</u>.

_____

d) Mutter wird ihrer <u>Tochter</u> ein Paket schicken.

_____

e) Herr Miller verkaufte Herrn Braun sein <u>Auto</u>.

_____

f) Mary bot ihrer Freundin eine Tasse <u>Tee</u> an.

_____

g) Herr Traynor gibt <u>Paul</u> 10 Pfund.

_____

h) Könntest du mir bitte den <u>Zucker</u> reichen?

_____

i) Onkel Henry schenkt George zum Geburtstag ein <u>Fahrrad</u>.

_____

j) Kannst du deiner Tante nicht eine <u>Postkarte</u> schreiben?

_____

k) Der Lehrer wird <u>den Schülern</u> die Aufgabe erklären.

_____

Wichtige unregelmäßige Verben (= irregular verbs)

Infinifiv	Simple Past	Partizip Perfekt	deutsche Bedeutung
be	was, were	been	sein
bear	bore	borne	tragen
beat	beat	beaten	schlagen
become	became	become	werden
begin	began	begun	beginnen
bend	bent	bent	biegen
bind	bound	bound	binden
bite	bit	bitten	beißen
blow	blew	blown	blasen
break	broke	broken	brechen
bring	brought	brought	bringen
build	built	built	bauen
buy	bought	bought	kaufen
cast	cast	cast	werfen
catch	caught	caught	fangen
choose	chose	chosen	wählen
come	came	come	kommen
cost	cost	cost	kosten
creep	crept	crept	kriechen
cut	cut	cut	schneiden
deal	dealt	dealt	(be)handeln
dig	dug	dug	graben
do	did	done	tun
draw	drew	drawn	ziehen, zeichnen
drink	drank	drunk	trinken
drive	drove	driven	fahren, treiben
eat	ate	eaten	essen
fall	fell	fallen	fallen
feed	fed	fed	füttern
feel	felt	felt	fühlen
fight	fought	fought	kämpfen
find	found	found	finden
flee	fled	fled	fliehen
forget	forgot	forgotten	vergessen
fly	flew	flown	fliegen
freeze	froze	frozen	frieren

☐ get	got	got	bekommen
☐ give	gave	given	geben
☐ go	went	gone	gehen
☐ grow	grew	grown	wachsen
☐ hang	hung	hung	hängen
☐ have	had	had	haben
☐ hear	heard	heard	hören
☐ hide	hid	hidden	verstecken
☐ hit	hit	hit	schlagen
☐ hold	held	held	halten
☐ hurt	hurt	hurt	verletzen
☐ keep	kept	kept	halten
☐ know	knew	known	kennen, wissen
☐ lay	laid	laid	legen
☐ lead	led	led	führen
☐ leave	left	left	verlassen
☐ lend	lent	lent	leihen
☐ let	let	let	lassen
☐ lie	lay	lain	liegen
☐ lose	lost	lost	verlieren
☐ make	made	made	machen, tun
☐ mean	meant	meant	meinen, bedeuten
☐ meet	met	met	treffen
☐ pay	paid	paid	zahlen
☐ put	put	put	stellen, legen
☐ read	read	read	lesen
☐ ride	rode	ridden	fahren, reiten
☐ ring	rang	rung	läuten
☐ rise	rose	risen	sich erheben, aufgehen
☐ run	ran	run	laufen, rennen
☐ say	said	said	sagen
☐ see	saw	seen	sehen
☐ seek	sought	sought	suchen
☐ sell	sold	sold	verkaufen
☐ send	sent	sent	senden, schicken
☐ set	set	set	setzen
☐ shake	shook	shaken	schütteln
☐ shine	shone	shone	scheinen
☐ shoot	shot	shot	schießen

☐ show	showed	shown	zeigen
☐ shut	shut	shut	schließen
☐ sing	sang	sung	singen
☐ sit	sat	sat	sitzen
☐ sleep	slept	slept	schlafen
☐ slide	slid	slid	gleiten
☐ speak	spoke	spoken	sprechen
☐ speed	sped	sped	eilen
☐ spell	spelt	spelt	buchstabieren
☐ spend	spent	spent	ausgeben, verbringen
☐ spread	spread	spread	verbreiten
☐ spring	sprang	sprung	springen
☐ stand	stood	stood	stehen
☐ steal	stole	stolen	stehlen
☐ stick	stuck	stuck	ankleben
☐ strike	struck	struck	schlagen
☐ swear	swore	sworn	fluchen, schwören
☐ sweep	swept	swept	fegen
☐ swim	swam	swum	schwimmen
☐ swing	swung	swung	schwingen
☐ take	took	taken	nehmen
☐ teach	taught	taught	lehren
☐ tear	tore	torn	zerreißen
☐ tell	told	told	erzählen
☐ think	thought	thought	denken
☐ throw	threw	thrown	werfen
☐ understand	understood	understood	verstehen
☐ wake	woke	woken	aufwecken, aufwachen
☐ wear	wore	worn	tragen
☐ weave	wove	woven	weben
☐ weep	wept	wept	weinen
☐ win	won	won	gewinnen
☐ wind	wound	wound	aufziehen, winden
☐ write	wrote	written	schreiben

Alphabetisches Wörterverzeichnis für die deutsch-englischen Übersetzungen

Abend	evening	entschuldigen	to apologise
abhalten	to hold	s. erinnern	to remember
ärgerlich	angry	s. erkälten	to catch a cold
Angst haben	to be afraid	erreichen	to reach
ängstlich	anxious	erwarten	to expect
allein	alone	erzählen	to tell
amüsieren	to amuse	erzielen	to score
ankommen	to arrive	essen	to eat
anrufen	to phone, to call	Essen	food
anschauen	to look at		
anweisen	to instruct	**Fabrik**	factory
Arbeit	work	fahren	to go, to drive
arbeiten	to work	Fahrplan	time-table
Arbeiter	worker	falsch	wrong
arbeitslos	unemployed	Familie	family
aufbringen	to raise	fast	almost
aufgeregt	excited	Ferien	holidays
aufmachen	to open	finden	to find
aufregend	exciting	fliegen	to fly
Augenblick	moment	fließend	fluent
Ausflug	trip	Flugzeug	plane
ausgehen	to go out	Fluß	river
ausgezeichnet	excellent	Fortschritt	progress
Auskunft	information	fragen	to ask
ausmachen	to mind	Frau	woman
ausprobieren	to try	s. freuen auf	to look forward to
Außenbezirk(e)	outskirts	Freundin	girl-friend
aussteigen	to get off	Friseur	hairdresser
Ausweis	passport	froh sein	to be glad
Auto	car	fühlen	to feel
		s. fürchten	to be afraid of
Bäcker	baker		
bauen	to build	**geben**	to give
bedienen	to serve	geboren werden	to be born
s. bedienen	to help oneself	gebraucht	used
bekommen	to get	Geburtstag	birthday
beliebt	popular	genau	exact, precise
Berg	mountain	gehen	to go, to walk
Besatzung	crew	gehören	to belong to
besuchen	to visit	Gepäck	luggage
Besucher	visitor	gern tun	to like to do
blau	blue	Geld	money
brauchen	to need	Geldbeutel	purse
Brief	letter	Gemüsehändler	grocer
Briefmarke	stamp	Geschäft	business; shop
bringen	to bring	Geschäftsleitung	management
Brot	bread	Geschenk	present
Bruder	brother	Geschichte	story
Brücke	bridge	gestern	yesterday
		gewinnen	to win
Deutsch	German	gewöhnen an	to get used to
Direktor	headmaster	glücklich	happy
dürfen	may; to be	Großbritannien	Great Britain
	allowed to	großartig	great
		Großmutter	grandmother
endlich	finally	Grund	reason
Einwohner	inhabitant		
entladen	to unload	**Haare**	hair
entlassen	to dismiss	halb	half
		Hauptstadt	capital

heiraten	to marry	Nachbar	neighbour
Herbst	autumn	Nähe	neighbourhood
hervorragend	excellent	nehmen	to take
heute	today	neu	new
holen	to fetch	nett	nice
Hose	trousers	nirgends	nowhere
Hund	dog	Nummernschild	number plate
hungrig	hungry		
		Obst	fruit
immer	always	öffnen	to open
interessieren	to interest	Onkel	uncle
interviewen	to interview	operieren	to operate
Irland	Ireland	Ort	place
Jahr	year	Paar	pair
Junge	boy	Paket	parcel
		Passagier	passenger
kaputt	broken	Patient	patient
kaufen	to buy	plötzlich	suddenly
Kaufhaus	department store	prüfen	to examine, to test
kaum	hardly	Punkt	point
kennen	to know		
Kenntnisse	knowledge	Rad	bike
Kind	child	Rat	advice
Kinder	children	Rede	speech
Klasse	class, form	Regenschirm	umbrella
Klassenkamerad	classmate	reisen	to travel
klettern	to climb	Reklame	advertisement
Klingel	bell	rennen	to run
klingen	to sound	reparieren	to repair
knapp	short	riechen	to smell
konzentrieren	to concentrate	Ring	ring
Königin	queen	Rolle	part, role
können	can, to be able to	rufen	to call
köstlich	delicious	Ruhe bewahren	to keep calm
krank	ill	russisch	Russian
kühl	cool		
Kühlschrank	fridge	sagen	to say
		Samstag	Saturday
Land	country	sauber machen	to clean
landen	to land	scharf	sharp
Lärm	noise	Schauspieler	actor
laufend	regular	Schere	scissors
Läufer	runner	Schlafanzug	pyjamas
läuten	to ring	schlecht	bad
legen	to put	schließen	to shut
s. leisten	to afford	schmecken	to taste
lesen	to read	schmutzig	dirty
letzte, r, s	last	schnell	fast, quick
letztes Mal	last time	schon	already
Leute	people	schön	beautiful
Licht	light	Schottland	Scotland
Lotterie	lottery	Schrank	cupboard
		schrecklich	terrible
machen	to do, to make	schreiben	to write
Marsch	march, hike	Schuh	shoe
Meile	mile	Schule	school
Möbel	furniture	Schüler	pupil
mögen	to like	schwarz	black
morgen	tomorrow	schwer	hard
heute Morgen	this morning	schwimmen	to swim
Motor	engine	sehen	to see
müde	tired	sehr	very

Sessel	armchair	Urlaub	holiday
s. setzen	to sit down	Ursache	reason
sicher	certain, sure		
sitzen	to sit	verbessern	to correct
sogar	even	verbringen	to spend
Sonntag	Sunday	verkaufen	to sell
spät	late	Verkäufer	shop-assistant
Spaziergang	walk	verlieren	to lose
spielen	to play	s. verspäten	to be late
Stadt	town	verstehen	to understand
Stichprobe	spot check	Verwandter	relative
Strand	beach	verzollen	to declare
Straße	road, street	vielleicht	perhaps
Streik	strike	vorsichtig	careful
Stromausfall	power failure	vorstellen	to introduce
suchen	to look for		
Süden	South	waschen	to wash
surfen	to surf	Wein	wine
Surfbrett	surfboard	Welle	wave
		wenig	little
Tag	day	wichtig	important
täglich	daily	wieder	again
Tennisschläger	racket	wiegen	to weigh
teuer	expensive	wissen	to know
treffen	to meet	Woche	week
Treffen	meeting	Wochenende	weekend
Treppe	staircase	wohnen	to live
		wollen	to want
U-Bahn	underground	wunderbar	wonderful
überall	everywhere		
überrascht	surprised	zeigen	to show
übersetzen	to translate	Zeit	time
Übersetzung	translation	Zeitung	newspaper
umdrehen	to turn	ziemlich	rather
Umgebung	surroundings	Zucker	sugar
ungefähr	about	Zug	train

Grammatikquiz

A

● 1. Welche Substantive haben nur die Singularform:
knowledge, office, neighbour, furniture, progress?

_____

● 2. Welche Substantive haben nur die Pluralform:
trousers, jackets, jeans, sweaters, tights?

_____

B

● Welches der folgenden Wörter – **any, each, every** – heißt jeder
beliebige?

_____

C

● 1. Wie lauten die Reflexivpronomen?

_____

_____

● 2. Wie heißen die reziproken Pronomen?

_____

Verbessere: 3. We could see us in the mirror.

_____

4. Tony hurt hisself.

_____

5. Help yourself, boys.

_____

6. I enjoyed me at the party.

_____

D ● 1. Nenne 5 Adverbien, die die gleiche Form wie die entsprechenden Adjektive haben.

_____

● 2. Übersetze folgende Adverbien:

kaum: _____   in letzter Zeit: _____

fast: _____   hart: _____

● 3. Wie heißen die Steigerungsformen?

fast: _____

happily: _____

F ● 1. Wie bildest du das Present Perfect Progressive?

_____

● 2. Wie bildest du das Past Perfect?

_____

G ● 1. Bilde das Future Progressive von: I am writing.

_____

● 2. Setze ins Future Perfect: They will play.

_____

Verbessere: 3. We will have do it.

_____

4. What have you been done all the time?

_____

5. Will you be visit your uncle tomorrow?

_____

● 1. Welche der folgenden Ausdrücke stehen im Passiv? Nenne bei diesen auch die Zeit:
you are asked, you have asked, you are inviting, you will be invited, you will have invited, you have been invited, you are being invited.

_____

_____

● 2. Womit kannst du den Urheber einer Handlung im Passiv anführen?

_____

● 3. Nach welchen der folgenden Verben folgt die -ing Form:
enjoy, want, avoid, mind, hope?

_____

● 4. Nenne 6 Verben mit Präpositionen, nach denen die -ing Form folgt:

_____

● 5. Verkürze folgenden Satz mithilfe eines Infinitivs:
Bob didn't know what he could do.

_____

Verbessere: 6. I want that he goes home.

_____

7. I don't know how to should ask.

_____

8. Do you mind to wait for me?

_____

9. The bridge is just be built.

_____

157

I ● 1. Übersetze: He may be in London.

_____

He might have missed the last bus.

_____

He would come. _____

He would have come. _____

K ● 1. Nenne die 3 Grundmuster bei den Bedingungssätzen:

Typ 1: if-Satz _____ Hauptsatz _____

Typ 2: if-Satz _____ Hauptsatz _____

Typ 3: if-Satz _____ Hauptsatz _____

● 2. Wann kannst du das Relativpronomen **who** bzw. **that** weglassen?

_____

● 3. Wann nimmst du bei der indirekten Rede **if** oder **whether**?

_____

● 4. Welche Zeitenverschiebung tritt ein, wenn das einleitende Verb im Past steht?

Present → _____, Past → _____ oder _____

will → _____, must → _____, can → _____

Verbessere: 5. This is the girl lives next door.

_____

6. Jack asked Bill if he didn't played tennis.

_____

7. Bill said that he must answer the letter.

_____

158

SCHWERPUNKTE DER SCHULAUFGABEN

Die 10 Schulaufgaben wurden in verschiedenen Klassen erprobt.
Wähle bitte die für dich zutreffenden Arbeiten aus.

● Die Schwerpunkte der Grammatik sind bei jeder Schulaufgabe angegeben.

1. Schulaufgabe aus dem Englischen

● some / any, everybody / everything ● Past Tense / Past Perfect
● Present Perfect

1.

Fill in 'some', 'any', 'anybody', 'everybody', 'everything', 'everywhere', 'each'.

a) Last month Jim and his mother went to New York to buy _____ clothes.

b) _____ of the buses was crowded.

c) _____ seemed to be travelling into the city.

d) When they arrived in New York, they didn't have _____ time to go shopping.

e) So they looked _____ for a hotel.

f) After _____ time they found a nice place near 5th Avenue.

g) Unfortunately there wasn't _____ to carry their luggage.

h) Next morning they had _____ coffee for breakfast, but they

   didn't get _____ fresh bread.

i) At first _____ seemed to go badly, but in the afternoon

   they were lucky enough to find _____ nice shops.

j) _____ of the shop-assistants was very friendly and helped

   to find them _____ they wanted.

160

1. Schulaufgabe aus dem Englischen

2.
Past Tense or Past Perfect?

a) After nobody (come) _____ for three days, Peter and

John suddenly (hear) _____ a bang.

b) At first they (not know) _____ what (cause) _____

that noise, but as soon as they (see) _____ the red

light, they (know) _____ that something (go) _____

_____ wrong.

c) As they (be) _____ not sure if someone (see) _____

_____ their bikes outside, they (decide) _____ to

leave the house.

d) A few minutes after they (close) _____ the door, they

quickly (run) _____ away.

3.
Since or for?

a) I have been going to school _____ seven years.

b) We have been learning English _____ the fifth year.

c) We have been learning French _____ the beginning of this year.

d) We have been learning it _____ three months now.

161

4.
Translation

a) Als Jim nach Florida kam, war er froh, im warmen Süden zu sein.

_____

_____

b) Er hatte noch nie gesurft, aber er war nicht ängstlich.

_____

_____

c) „Hast du kein Surfbrett? Du kannst unseres nehmen", sagte ein Nachbar.

_____

_____

d) „Ich könnte dich zum Strand bringen."

_____

e) „Oh, fein, dann werden wir morgen alle zum Strand gehen."

_____

_____

f) „Wenn die Wellen zu hoch sind, lege ich mich auf das Brett."

_____

_____

2. Schulaufgabe aus dem Englischen

● Adjektiv/Adverb   ● Wortstellung   ● Past Perfect/Simple Past
● modale Hilfsverben

1.
Adjective or Adverb?

Jack and Sylvia Murphy entered the room _____ (noisy).

They saw their parents sitting there _____ (quiet), but

looking rather _____ (unhappy).

Sylvia: Mum, what's the matter? Why do you feel _____ (sad)?

                  Did Jack not work _____ (good) at school?

Jack: Stop it. I've _____ (real) worked _____
                  (hard) this year.

Mr Murphy looked at his family _____ (sad).

Mr Murphy: Now listen _____ (careful). I'm on strike.

                  We don't get _____ (good) wages, so the dockers are

                  getting _____ (angry). The management told us

                  that we don't work _____ (fast) enough. They think

                  they can _____ (easy) sack every fifth man.

Mrs Murphy: I'm also _____ (real, disappointed).

                  Things are getting _____ (bad). I _____
                  (hard) know what to do.

2. Schulaufgabe aus dem Englischen

2.

Put the verb in brackets into Simple Past. Write the direct and indirect objects as pronouns.

a) Jill wanted to hear Grandpa's story again.

He _____ (tell).

b) John wanted to have the potatoes.

His mother _____ (pass).

c) Peter wanted to learn the new German sentences.

His sister _____ (teach).

d) The Smiths wanted to buy the Brown's car.

Yesterday they _____ (sell).

e) Mary Potter wanted some blouses.

Mrs Garner _____ (send) for her birthday.

3.

Past Perfect or Simple Past?

a) After Mr Miller _____ the car park, he _____
   to the baker's.   (leave/go)

b) He _____ in town that day two hours earlier, but he

   _____ to buy some bread.   (be/forget)

c) After he _____ the bread, he _____
   back to the car park.   (buy/hurry)

d) He _____ the car after he _____
   for the ticket.   (start/pay)

2. Schulaufgabe aus dem Englischen

4.
Translate into English.

a) Die Schule konnte Tennisschläger kaufen, weil die Schüler viel Geld aufge-
bracht hatten. Alle Schüler durften sie ausprobieren.

_____

_____

b) Wenn du mir die Daumen drückst, werde ich vielleicht 15 Punkte erzielen.

_____

_____

c) Die Millers können es sich nicht leisten, einen Ausflug zu machen, weil sie
arbeitslos und sehr knapp an Geld sind.

_____

_____

d) Ihr dürft nicht erwarten allein zu sein, wenn ihr zu einem beliebten Ort auf dem
Land fahrt.

_____

_____

e) Die Geschäftsleitung musste viele Arbeiter entlassen. Aus diesem Grund gab
es einen Streik, den der Direktor nicht haben wollte.

_____

_____

_____

3. Schulaufgabe aus dem Englischen

● vermischte Zeiten ● Fragebildung ● modale Hilfsverben
● Passiv

1.
Put in the right tenses.

Two months ago David Owen (to meet) _____ a beautiful girl

and he (to invite) _____ her to the cinema.

After they (to see) _____ the new Woody Allen film, they (to go) _____

to a bar in London's West End. They (to talk) _____ and

(to dance) _____ a lot, and it (to be) _____ already late at night

when the girl (to say) _____ to David who (to be) _____

a famous tennis player: "Oh David, don't drink so much! If you (to drink)

_____ so much whisky and soda now, you (to lose)

_____ your match tomorrow." "Don't worry", (to answer)

_____ David, "I (to eat) _____ my Müsli

tomorrow and this keeps me in form."

2.
Find the questions.

a) _____ ?
No, safety-belts needn't be put on all the time.

b) _____ ?
No, radios mustn't be played during the flight.

166

Englisch
Grammatik im Lernsystem
Band 3

H. Gumtau und W. Kurschatke

Lösungsheft

MANZ VERLAG

Schwerpunkte der Grammatik

1.
a) Saturdays, shops, schools b) boys, girls, school c) men, women, weekends d) weekday, things, shops e) potatoes, tomatoes, apples, peaches, plums, carrots, strawberries, things f) children, parents g) sorts, vegetables, flowers, bushes, trees, friends

2.
a) Billy has a poor knowledge of geography. b) Tony makes good progress at school. c) Has Sally already done her homework? d) The information about the meeting is very important. e) The doctor gave Tom a good piece of advice. f) The furniture in our house is very old. g) My aunt gave us some furniture last year. h) An armchair is a piece of furniture you can sit on. i) The information Peter gave me was wrong.

3.
a) Bill's trousers are very dirty. b) He needs a new pair of trousers. c) Jane wears glasses. d) She can't find her glasses. e) These scissors are not very sharp. f) I'd like to buy two pairs of good scissors. g) These tights are too big. h) I need a new pair of tights, two pairs of shorts, three shirts and a pair of pyjamas. i) My friend lives in the outskirts of London. j) Many thanks for your letter.

4.
a) today's paper b) an hour's rest c) the newsagent's, this week's magazine d) month's wait, their uncle's e) the grocer's, the butcher's f) Foyle's, Woolworth's g) today's weather forecast h) day's work i) chemist's

5.
Lisa buys fruit at the greengrocer's and bread at the baker's. b) Laura spends a week's holiday at her uncle's in Wales. c) This is yesterday's paper. Have you seen today's? d) Every Sunday the Smith family makes an hours' walk. e) You can buy the exercise-book at the stationer's. f) For Heaven's sake, Johnny, you must go to the barber's. Your hair is too long.

6.
parents, Scottish, week's, beautiful, islands, sites, advertisements, There, children's, arcades, people's, parents', quite, grocer's, ourselves

7.
a) anyone, anywhere, somewhere, someone b) anywhere, something, someone, some c) any, none, somewhere d) some, some, some, any, some

8.

a) every b) each c) everything, every d) everywhere, each, each e) Each
f) everything g) everywhere, everyone, Each, any h) Everyone i) Every, every

9.

a) Each pupil in our class likes English. b) Every car needs a number plate. c) You
can see this advertisement everywhere. d) Everyone in our house is very nice.
e) Have you understood everything? f) Each of us knows the new film. g) Any person
in our club can use the ground. h) I'm sure that every child likes to play ball. i) We
saw someone swimming in the river. j) You could have asked each of them. k) Is
there any food left? – No, the boys have eaten everything up.

10.

a) My, you, me, yours, I, it, You, your b) you, my, I, I, mine c) You, my, you, yours
d) Our, yours e) my, I, them, I, you, them, your, you, them, you, mine f) they, yours,
they, mine, I, them

11.

a) himself b) herself c) themselves d) himself e) yourself f) itself g) yourself
h) themselves i) herself j) herself k) yourselves l) himself m) himself n) ourselves
o) themselves p) myself

12.

a) –, myself, – b) – c) themselves d) – e) –, – f) – g) ourselves h) myself i) themselves

13.

a) Where can we meet? b) If you are late, you must apologize c) Tony introduces
himself to his new boss. d) If you are interested in the book, you can read it yourself.
e) I can't get used to this noise. f) The children sit down and concentrate on their
work. g) Jenny is afraid of the wild dog. h) Sally and Jane amused themselves at
John's birthday party. i) Peter saw the queen herself in London.

14.

a) each other (one another) b) themselves c) yourselves d) each other e) herself
f) –, – g) each other h) each other i) – j) himself k) – l) each other m) herself n) yourself

15.

a) Nancy, please go and wash (yourself). b) The workers made themselves a cup
of tea. c) Mr W. felt very hungry. d) Tony could not remember anything. e) Sandra
suddenly turned round and looked at us. f) The bell is ringing. I'll go myself and open
the door myself. g) My brother knows that we don't like each other. h) The two teams

haven't played angainst each other for three years. i) Can you remember the last holidays? j) The dog and the cat were afraid of each other. k) Little Bill is afraid of the dog.

16.
a) difficult b) well c) carefully d) easily e) excellent f) fast g) correctly h) difficult, automatically i) nervous, politely j) easy, clearly, slowly

17.
a) The story of this film sounds exciting. b) Sarah felt wonderful. She became very excited. c) Her friend Peter kept cool. d) The food in the restaurant tasted delicious. e) The wine was warm. It smelled terrible. f) Peter got very angry. g) Sarah looked great. She just seemed a little tired. h) Peter and Sarah felt happy. i) It will soon get cold outside. j) Peter's idea didn't sound bad. k) Sarah didn't look surprised.

18.
a) fair, fairly, hardly, near, fairly, daily, late, late b) fast, high, early, far, long, late c) hard, nearly, fast, enough, nearly, enough

19.
a) The 8 o'clock train goes daily. b) My uncle Willi has got a fast car, but he doesn't drive fast. c) It is late, Tom. Go to bed. You must get up early tomorrow. d) Tom hardly has any time at the weekend. He nearly always has to work. He works very hard. e) Bob is a near relative of ours. He lives near us. f) The president didn't speak long. It wasn't a long speech. g) Ian speaks German fairly fluently. h) Mount Everest is a high mountain. The men climbed up high.

20.
a) hard, good, easily, beautiful, happy, fast b) late, quickly, carefully, slowly, nervous, angry, funny

21.
a) beautifully, more beautifully b) cleverly, more cleverly c) hard, harder d) early, earlier e) more carelessly, most carelessly f) little, less g) correctly, more correctly, most correctly h) well, better, best i) badly, worse, worst

22.
a) Richard is a fast runner. He runs faster than his classmates. b) Ch. Ch. was a wonderful actor. He played all his parts excellently. c) Mr. T. speaks Russian fluently, but he speaks German even better. d) J. H. is an excellent swimmer. He swims faster than T. C., but D. F. swims fastest. e) Mr Jones did the translation very precisely. He is a very good translator. f) G. eats less than her brother. Her grandma eats least.

5

23.
a) is having b) is beginning c) are you having, am having, have d) are you looking at, am looking at e) is just taking off f) barks, is making g) are you going, am going h) are the boys not doing, are listening

24.
a) Have you ever been, was b) has just arrived, have not met, rang, has known c) did you see, have not seen, met d) Have you had, had e) have you done, went, didn't clean, came f) Have you seen, haven't seen

25.
a) Have you already written the letter? – Yes, I wrote it last night. b) When did your train arrive? – It arrived at ten today. c) Jim lost his purse yesterday and hasn't found it yet. d) Have you ever been to Ireland? – Yes, we were there last summer. e) When did you see Paul for the last time? – I haven't met him for a year. f) Diana has been ill for three days. She caught a cold last weekend.

26.
a) has Tom been waiting, – has been waiting for b) have your parents been living, have been living, since c) have you and Paul been writing, have been writing to each other for d) has Ian been speaking, has been speaking, for e) have your friends been staying, have been staying, for f) has it been raining, has been raining, since g) have these pupils been learning, have been learning English for

27.
a) have not had, have never been b) have always wanted, have bought c) have been looking for, haven't seen d) have been living, haven't been, you have been reading e) have been reading

28.
a) Tom and Susan are just sitting in the cafe. b) How long have you been living in this town? We have been living here since 1996. c) And how long has your father been working in that factory? He has been working there for two years. d) How long have you had this beautiful ring? I've had it since my last birthday. e) Have you ever been to Yorkshire? No, I've never been there. I've always wanted to visit the Yorkshire Moors. f) I've been reading a book about the North of England for two weeks.

29.
a) had worked b) had read c) had started d) had gone e) had arrived f) had heard

g) had scored h) had got i) had done j) had not eaten k) had taken off l) had forgotten
m) had finished n) had stolen

30.
a) After he had gone to the Tower, he visited Madame Tussaud's. b) After he had
done some shopping in Oxford Street, he went to a cinema in Soho. c) After he had
visited the Zoo, he had a meal at a Chinese restaurant. d) After he had looked at
paintings in the National Gallery, he listened to an open-air concert. e) After he had
seen the Changing of the Guard, he met his girl-friend Susy. f) After he had paid
for his room, he took the next train to Dover.

31.
a) had Mr Traynor known, married b) met, had lived c) told, had seen, had liked
d) had introduced, became e) went, had been f) had arrived, wrote, told g) had
taught, went h) had stayed, returned i) had finished, moved

32.
a) will be b) won't be able to c) are we going to do d) are going to have, are not going
to stay, are going to sleep e) are we going to do f) will walk g) will we h) will be able,
will be

33.
a) At 9 o'clock they will be getting their bikes ready. b) At 9.30 they will be setting
off . . . c) At 12.30 they will be having a picnic . . . d) For the night they will be staying
. . . e) In the evening they will be sitting together and will be singing songs. f) On
Sunday morning they will be going to church. g) At noon they will be returning home.

34.
a) will you be doing, will be staying b) will be swimming c) will be leaving d) will be
staying e) will be landing f) won't be having g) Will you be going h) will be raining
i) will be doing j) will be writing k) will be studying l) will be waiting m) will be swimming

35.
a) will have passed b) will have done c) will have left d) will have read e) will have
lived f) will have repaired g) will have started h) will have finished i) will have travelled
j) will have answered k) will have seen

36.
a) I am leaving for London next week. b) Jenny and I are going to a film at 7.30.
c) Are you going to Leeds tomorrow? d) Bill is playing tennis with me this afternoon.
e) The cafe is closing in half an hour. f) My sister is getting married in summer.

g) We are not going to Stockport next Sunday. h) They are playing Beethoven tonight. i) John is flying to Paris this weekend.

37.
a) are spending b) has not been, is enjoying c) visited d) could not, was e) took, went f) started, had told, to be g) was h) was shining, were eating i) heard j) had lost, had fallen, was not k) ran, had heard l) was able to pull m) are, were not n) have never felt, said, had saved o) will . . . do p) won't be, will be able q) will hire, will just lie r) will have seen s) is, will come

38.
a) are planted b) are repaired c) is checked d) are sold e) are worn f) are . . . picked g) is kept h) are driven i) are put on j) is played k) is visited l) are built m) is spoken n) is watched o) are read

39.
a) must be milked . . . b) ought to be cut . . . c) A plough has to be repaired . . . d) The tractor could be cleaned . . . e) A fence should be repaired first . . . f) A field must be ploughed . . . g) Potatoes have to be planted . . . h) The garden can be dug . . .

40.
a) was knocked down b) was called c) was taken d) was carried e) was put f) was operated g) was bandaged h) was taken i) was visited j) was interviewed k) was questioned l) was sent

41.
a) The flowers will be watered. b) The windows will be cleaned. c) Tom's bike will be repaired. d) Questions will be asked. e) Dinner will be cooked. f) All my money will be stolen. g) The exercises will be done. h) The camera will be smashed. i) The match will be played. j) A new supermarket will be opened.

42.
a) My father's car has been repaired . . . b) A million pounds have been stolen . . . c) This room has been cleaned this week. d) Tony has not been invited to our party. e) Barbara's bike has not been found yet. f) The Brown's cat has been run over by a lorry. g) The windows have been broken by the boys. h) Smoking has not been allowed in schools.

43.
a) The bike had been stolen. b) The air had been let out . . . c) The door had been damaged. d) Some beer bottles had been dropped . . . e) The tickets had been sold.

f) England had been conquered . . . g) The roads had been blocked. h) The football match had been postponed. i) The Spanish Armada had been defeated . . . j) Two pedestrians had been injured. k) A new president had been chosen.

44.
a) The road is being repaired. b) You are being called. c) I was being served. d) The bridges were being built. e) Alan is being examined. f) The minister was being interviewed. g) The meeting was being held. h) The patient is being operated on. i) We were being asked. j) The engines are being improved. k) These houses were being built.

45.
a) Are all suitcases checked? b) Our suitcases can be opened. c) They didn't open my bag last time. d) A pistol has just been found by an officer. e) They will search that man carefully. f) Does an officer take away his passport? g) He can be sent to prison, can't he? h) If they had not found the pistol, other people might have been killed by the man. i) Were the diamonds found? j) The plane is unloaded and the tanks are filled up by these men.

46.
a) When a plane has landed, it is unloaded. b) Will the luggage be weighed? Yes, it will. After the luggage has been weighed, it must be taken to the plane and must be loaded in. c) If spot checks are made, the passengers must show their passports. d) 20 bottles of wine had to be declared. e) Last time Mr Miller was not checked. f) After the luggage had been checked, it was taken to the hall. g) One of the planes is being unloaded by some workers.

47.
a) being b) opening c) driving d) dancing e) laughing f) walking, going, taking g) telling h) going i) smoking, eating j) buying k) flying

48.
a) on doing b) up trying c) for working d) about helping e) of doing f) of becoming g) to writing

49.
a) Paul was proud of winning . . . b) Angela is good at playing . . . c) Pamela is fond of riding horses. d) David is afraid of going out when it's dark. e) Stanley is interested in reading . . . f) Barbara's mother is tired of telling her . . . g) Georgie was ashamed of making . . .

50.

a) Hans has the chance of learning English at school. b) Hans has the opportunity of living in Scotland for a year. c) Mr Brown is in danger of losing his money. d) Instead of flying to Scotland, Hans goes by ferry. e) After finding the cheapest way, Hans booked his ticket. f) Before telling Helga about his plans, he invited her for a coffee. g) After saying good-bye to all his friends, he left.

51.

a) Hast du jemals (schon einmal) daran gedacht, dein Land zu verlassen? b) Ja, ich würde mich dafür interessieren, fremde Länder zu sehen. c) Kannst du dir vorstellen, für viele Jahre in einem anderen Land zu leben? d) Nun, ich möchte nicht jahrelang im Ausland leben. e) Aber könntest du nicht daran denken, für eine kürzere Zeit zu gehen? f) Ja. Nachdem ich meine Prüfungen bestanden habe, wäre ich darauf aus, Teile Südamerikas zu sehen. g) Es würde dir vielleicht gefallen, dort zu arbeiten. h) Ja. Ich träume davon, eine gute Arbeit zu bekommen. So würde es mir nichts ausmachen, einige Zeit dort zu verbringen.

52.

a) They don't know how to get to Reading. b) ... who to ask c) ... when to catch ... d) ... what to bring ... e) ... how to get ... f) ... where to meet ... g) ... who to ask ... h) ... where to buy ... i) ... which train to take ...

53.

a) how to get b) where to cross c) when to go d) how to pronounce e) when to get up f) how to use g) what to wear h) where to buy i) how to bake j) who to ask k) how to ride l) where to get m) what to do

54.

a) Clara ist nicht sicher, was sie zu Jills Party anziehen soll. b) Die Pfadfinder fanden heraus, wie sie den Fluss überqueren konnten. c) Die Kinder hatten keine Ahnung, was sie am Wochenende tun sollten. d) Mein Freund sagte mir, wann ich ihn am Bahnhof treffen könnte. e) John weiß nicht, wen er um Hilfe fragen kann. f) Er zögert, welchen Bus er nehmen soll. g) Margaret fragte sich, wo sie Briefmarken kaufen konnte. h) Könnten Sie mir sagen, wie ich zum Rathaus komme? i) Man sagte Herrn Smith, wann er anfangen sollte zu arbeiten. j) Als Herr Clark ankam, wusste er nicht, wo er seinen Mantel aufhängen sollte.

55.

a) Bob was happy to hear that ... b) C. was the first man to discover ... c) ... the best pub to have lunch? d) ... the last to arrive ... e) ... the next pupil to be examined. f) Mr Brown was sorry to read about the accident. g) . . . the oldest man to take part in . . . h) We were surprised to see our friends again. i) Nick is too lazy to help his father.

56.

a) Tom doesn't want his brother to run away. b) He wanted him to stay at home. c) I want you to shut the door. d) Why do you want me to do all the work alone? e) Mrs K. would like John to visit his uncle. f) Would you like Jean to call you on Sunday? g) The children want their grandmother to tell them a story. h) Mrs J. would like her son to marry her friend's daughter.

57.

a) Peter has not been able to come. b) Will Jane be able to answer? c) Ian had to stay at home yesterday. d) Alan will have to get up early tomorrow morning. e) Tony was not allowed to visit his friends. f) Mrs Miller didn't have to wait long. g) Will we have to work at the weekend? h) Bill had not been able to call us. i) Mr Brown has had to sell his car.

58.

a) was able to buy a camera b) couldn't/wasn't able to play tennis c) couldn't/wasn't able to open the door d) was able to post the letter e) could/was able to hear the birds f) could/was able to see the match g) couldn't/wasn't able to think properly h) couldn't/weren't able to walk far i) was able to run the marathon j) was able to check his maths homework k) was able to show films l) couldn't/wasn't able to jump over the wall m) were able to understand the announcer

59.

a) might b) mightn't c) might have d) mightn't e) might f) might have g) mightn't h) might i) might have j) might k) might l) mightn't

60.

a) Spiele im Fußballtoto, Peter, du gewinnst vielleicht ein paar Pfund. b) Rufe zuerst Barbara an. Sie ist möglicherweise nicht zu Hause. Sie könnte vielleicht nach Liverpool gefahren sein. c) Die Millers sind heute Abend nicht zu Hause. Sie sind vielleicht ins Kino gegangen. d) Peters Mannschaft ist ärgerlich, weil sie das Spiel verloren haben. Sie hätten vielleicht gewinnen können, wenn sie wirkungsvoller gespielt hätten. e) Wenn Susy auf das Baby aufpasst, können die Eltern vielleicht einen langen Spaziergang machen. f) Wir wissen noch nicht, was wir heute Nachmittag tun sollen, aber wir könnten vielleicht in den Jugendclub gehen.

61.

a) I would call the police. b) Jenny wouldn't walk in the rain. c) A used bike wouldn't be as expensive as a new one. d) A taxi would have been very expensive. e) The girls would have read the paper. f) Would you visit us at the weekend? g) Nick and Bill will ask their uncle next week. h) They won't go by train. i) Would they have read the time-table? j) They would take the next bus. k) Their uncle would have told them l) Their aunt would be at home.

62.

a) ought to b) oughtn't to c) ought to d) oughtn't to e) ought to f) ought to, oughtn't to g) ought to have h) Oughtn't . . . to i) ought to have j) ought to k) Ought . . . to

63.

a) Billy sollte nicht jedes Wort glauben, das sein Freund sagt. b) Du bist alt genug, Sandra. Du solltest es besser wissen. c) Hätten wir die Reifen überprüfen sollen, bevor wir losfuhren? d) Du solltest deinen Vater nicht stören, wenn er schläft. e) Jeder sollte anhalten, wenn die Ampel rot ist. f) Die Leute sollten die ganze Zeit sorgfältig auf den Verkehr achten. g) Unfälle wie diese sollten nicht wieder passieren. h) Autofahrer sollten vor dem Fahren keinen Alkohol trinken. i) Jane hätte härter üben sollen.

64.

a) If it's rainy, the boys can't go skating. b) If Clara forgets her umbrella, she will get soaked to the skin c) If Peter has enough money, he will buy a new bike. d) If Betty is at home this afternoon, she will help her mother. e) If you eat too many sweets, you will spoil your teeth. f) If Jane is in London before noon, she will not miss the procession. g) If the dog barks, the baby will not be able to sleep. h) If Mrs Potter pays the bill in time, she won't have any trouble. i) If Mr Sleeve doesn't post the letter in time, it won't arrive before Monday.

65.

a) If the weather is fine, I'll go for a long walk. b) If I lose my way in London, I'll ask a policeman. c) If I miss my bus, I'll wait for the next one. d) If my tooth hurts, I'll go the dentist's, e) If I win £ 5000, I' ll give a big party. f) If I see a thief coming out of a house, I'll call the police. g) If I've got a headache, I'll take a tablet.

66.

a) would buy b) was c) would not make d) didn't wear e) broke down f) would spend g) wouldn't drink h) understood i) ate j) asked k) would you go shopping l) would get m) knew

67.

a) . . . left . . ., . . . would get . . . b) . . . went . . . would arive . . . c) . . . came . . . would come . . . d) . . . brought . . . would be able to sing . . . e) . . . came in time . . . could help f) . . . met . . . might ask . . . g) . . . was . . . would give h) . . . came . . . would have to make . . . i) was . . . would take place . . . j) . . . didn't arrive . . . could take . . . k) . . . helped . . . would be . . . l) . . . caught . . . would be . . .

68.

a) If Peter had been in town, he could have met his girl-friend. b) If the weather had been fine, the boys might have gone on a tour. c) If my father had given up smoking earlier, he wouldn't have become ill. d) If Paul had known that Janet was coming, he would have invited her to the cinema. e) If Martha had brought him the books, Mathew could have read them at the weekend.

69.

a) If Nicole had had time, she would have visited the Tower. b) If the old man had seen the car, he wouldn't have been run over. c) If the driver had fastened his safety belt, he wouldn't have been injured. d) If his son had known that he was in hospital, he would have visited him. e) If the driver had been careful enough, he wouldn't have had an accident. f) If he hadn't driven very fast, the accident wouldn't have been so bad.

70.

a) would buy b) hadn't bought c) will be allowed to d) offered e) is, won't go f) would have taken, had been g) will be h) is i) won't need to work j) had k) might have earned, had worked l) will, comes

71.

a) What would you do if you had a lot of money? b) If you had played in the lottery, you might have won 10 000 Marks. c) If your father gave you the money, you could buy a new bike. d) If I ask him, I'm sure he'll give me his. e) Tom could have helped you if he had wanted to. f) If we go to Scotland on holiday next summer, we can visit the Highlands. g) Mary would certainly come with us if she hadn't been there last year. (Beachte: Hier übst du eine andere Zeitenfolge!)

72.

a) who b) that c) that d) who e) who f) who g) who h) that i) that j) who k) who l) who m) that n) that o) who p) that q) who r) that

73.

a) The park that is on your right is Hyde Park. b) We listened to the guide who explained everything. c) This is the Tower that was a prison in former days. d) We are in a big street now that is called Fleet Street. e) On that column stands A.N. who was the hero of T. f) That building that you can see over there is B.P. g) The flag that is flying on the roof is the U.J. h) We've seen all the sights that I showed to you on the map.

74.

a) . . . whose ears . . . b) . . . whose faces . . . c) . . . whose feathers . . . d) . . . whose dresses . . . e) . . . whose necks . . . f) whose little ones . . . g) . . . whose skin . . . h) . . . whose teeth . . . i) . . . whose mothers . . .

75.

a) I need b) that you lent me c) whose book I still have d) he went to e) who lost his book f) who you met here g) I'm thinking of h) that my uncle drives i) who won the prize j) you met k) who cuts your hair

76.

a) Es gibt in Helgas Klasse ein Mädchen, dessen Vater Engländer ist. b) Ist das das Mädchen, das wir letzten Samstag in der Stadt trafen? c) Ja, und sie ist das Mädchen, dessen Bruder mein Freund ist. d) Das Haus, in dem sie leben, ist das größte in der Stadt. e) Das Mädchen, das Heidi heißt, besucht oft ihre Großeltern, die in Brighton leben. f) Ihre Großmutter ist nicht die Art von Frau, die nicht im Meer schwimmen würde. g) Letzten Sommer rettete sie das kleine Mädchen, dessen Eltern ihre Nachbarn sind. h) Es war das aufregendste Abenteuer, das Heidi jemals gehabt hatte.

77.

a) The doctor who Heidi's grandma phoned was a friend of the family. b) The neighbours whose car was broken couldn't fetch the child. c) Is this the house your grandparents live in? d) Where is the family who lived in this house? e) Heidi's grandma is a woman who knows everything better. f) Peter showed me the book he bought. g) It's the book whose story I know. h) The book (that) Peter bought is the most beautiful one I've ever read.

78.

a) Bob says (that) he is trying to finish the exercise. b) David asks if they are meeting in the evening. c) Clare says (that) she's been learning hard since September. d) Pamela says (that) she will work four months for her exam. e) She adds (that) her friend Bob helps her. f) George wants to know if Jack wants to join them. g) Clare says (that) their teacher is going to give them some books for their preparation. h) Pamela says (that) she has not told her father about it yet. i) George says (that) he needn't hurry because he's got a lot of time.

14

79.

a) Charles said (that) he had got the job and he was very happy about it. b) He said (that) he was/had been awfully sad that he was/had been out of work. c) Billy remarked (that) his uncle also worked in the factory. d) He said (that) he had always wanted to hear something about his job. e) Sheila said (that) she was playing the guitar at their party. f) She remarked (that) she was going to ask her brother to give her a lift. g) Anne declared (that) they told all their friends to go to the concert. h) Claire pointed out (that) she had never heard such lovely music.

80.

a) Nicole asked why Mrs K. liked to go to Germany. b) Jill wondered how long she had been planning her holidays. c) The children wanted to know if it was possible for them all to go on a tour. d) Mr K. asked when they were going to leave from Dover. e) He asked his wife if she got/had got the tickets. f) Maureen asked why she (they) hadn't booked a flight. g) Billy wanted to know where they could stay for the first night. h) Mother asked who had seen their big suitcase. i) Billy asked how long it took them to get to Calais. j) Mrs K. asked her husband if he thought he (they) could buy two bags.

81.

a) Tony said (that) he started/had started school nine years before. b) Paul remarked (that) Lizzie won/had won a prize the day before. c) Robert added (that) they would win their match the following day. d) Charles pointed out (that) he had to train harder because he was not fast enough. e) Fred shouted (that) they didn't have to be afraid because the others weren't too strong. f) Charles promised (that) they could support them the following Saturday. g) Bob said (that) they might learn a lot because they would get a very good coach. h) Charles remarked (that) they should try to get some more money. i) Frank pointed out (that) they could solve that problem and (that) that was exactly what their coach said.

82.

a) Maureen asked if they would be meeting their friends when they stayed in Munich b) Mother asked Billy if he had been learning enough German at school. c) The customs officer asked them if they had anything to declare. d) Mr Kenyon asked if they shouldn't phone the travel agents. e) The children asked what sort of train they could catch. f) Mr Kenyon wanted to know if they had to change trains at Cologne. g) Mrs Kenyon's friend asked how long their holidays would last. h) She asked her if they would be back at the end of August. i) She wanted to know who their friends were they would visit in Germany.

83.

a) What's the matter with you? b) I've had a cough for months and I can't get rid of it. c) Are you a heavy smoker? d) Yes, I am. I usually smoke five to ten cigarettes a day, but sometimes even as many as fifteen. e) Do you realize that smoking is extremely unhealthy? f) I don't mind; I'm still young. g) Have you ever tried to give up smoking? h) . . . I've tried it twice, but I haven't managed it.

84.

a) Where did Maureen and Bob go on holiday? b) Why did they travel by train? c) What did Bob buy before they started? d) When did they set off? e) How long did it take them to get to Carlisle? f) Who did they meet near Loch Lomond? g) What did he ask them? h) Who said 'good bye' to the old man after three days? i) For how many weeks did they stay in the Highlands? j) What did they find on their way to Aberdeen? k) When did Bob and Maureen return from their trip?

85.

a) Where does Mr Traynor come from? b) What was Uncle Henry talking about? c) What are a lot of people waiting for? d) What is cheese made from? e) What was Anne looking for all the time? f) Who was Mr Brown eating with in a Chinese restaurant? g) Who has the postman brought a parcel from? h) What is Bob very much interested in? i) What are all the mountains covered with? j) Who did Mrs Traynor send a Christmas card to in Austria? k) What school do Maureen and Kate go to in Reading?

86.

a) Who did you get the letter from? b) Who does this umbrella belong to? c) What is Susy afraid of? d) Do you know what John is looking for? e) Who did the Millers spend their holiday with last year? f) Who has Mother bought a nice birthday present for? g) What can Bob clean his shoes with? h) Who were the people talking about yesterday? i) Who does that big car over there belong to? j) What are the children looking for?

87.

a) The Müllers will spend their next holiday in England. b) They are going to hire a boat on a canal in Cheshire. c) It is fairly easy to steer a boat. d) Herr Müller has already booked a boat in Chester. e) The children are waiting for the start impatiently. f) In the evenings they can go to a pub for a drink.

88.

a) Last week Bob sent his girlfriend a letter. b) Betty wrote a postcard to her grandparents. c) The postman brings Mr Brown a parcel. d) Grandma told the children a story. e) Tom showed his camera to Clara, not to Betty. f) Mr. Miller sold his old car to the car dealer. g) Ian sent Jean a telegram. h) Mrs Smith passed her husband the salt. i) The manager offered a ticket to his friends, not to everyone.

89.
a) Peter gave Betty the book, not the exercise-book. b) Betty wrote the letter to Max, not to his sister. c) Tony showed Jean his stamps. d) Mother will send a parcel to her daughter. e) Mr Miller sold Mr Brown his car. f) Mary offered her girl-friend a cup of tea. g) Mr Traynor gives £ 10 to Paul. h) Could you pass me the sugar, please? i) Uncle Henry gives George a bike for his birthday. j) Can't you write your aunt a postcard? k) The teacher will explain the exercise to the pupils.

Grammatikquiz

A 1. knowledge, furniture, progress 2. trousers, jeans, tights
B any
C 1. siehe S. 29 2. siehe S. 34 3. We could see ourselves in the mirror. 4. Tony hurt himself. 5. Help yourselves, boys. 6. I enjoyed myself at the party.
D 1. siehe S. 40 2. hardly, lately, nearly, hard 3. faster, fastest; more happily, most happily
F 1. siehe S. 50 2. siehe S. 55
G 1. I will be writing 2. They will have played 3. We will have done it. 4. What have you been doing all the time? 5. Will you be visiting our uncle tomorrow?
H 1. you are asked (Present), you will be invited (Future), you have been invited (Present Perfect), you are being invited (Present Progressive) 2. by 3. enjoy, avoid, mind 4. siehe S. 87 5. Bob didn't know what to do. 6. I want him to go home. 7. I don't know how to ask. 8. Do you mind waiting for me? 9. The bridge is just being built.
I Er ist vielleicht in London. Er hat möglicherweise den letzten Bus versäumt. Er würde kommen. Er wäre gekommen.
K 1. siehe S. 112, 115, 118 2. Wenn es Objekt des Relativsatzes ist. 3. Bei Yes-/No-Fragen (deutsch: ob) 4. Past, Past . . . Past Perfect, would, had to, could 5. This is the girl who lives next door. 6. Jack asked Bill if if he didn't play tennis. 7. Bill said that he had to answer the letter.

Schwerpunkte der Schulaufgaben

1. Schulaufgabe

1.
a) some b) Each c) Everybody d) any e) everywhere f) some g) anybody h) some, any i) everything, some j) Each, everything

2.
a) had come, heard b) didn't know, had caused, had seen, knew, had gone c) were, had seen, decided d) had closed, ran

3.
a) for b) since c) since d) for

4.
a) When Jim came to Florida, he was glad to be in the warm South. b) He had never surfed before, but he was not afraid. c) 'Haven't you got a surfboard? You can take ours', said a neighbour d) 'I could take you to the beach.' e) 'Oh, fine, then we'll all go to the beach tomorrow.' f) 'If the waves are too high, I'll lie on the board.'

2. Schulaufgabe

1.
noisily, quietly, unhappy, sad, well, really, hard, sadly, carefully, good, angry, fast, easily, really, disappointed, worse, hardly

2.
a) He told her it again. b) His mother passed them to him. c) His sister taught him them. d) Yesterday they sold it to them. e) Mrs Gerner sent them to her for her birthday.

3.
a) had left, went b) had been, forgot c) had bought, hurried d) started, had pald

4.
a) The school was able to buy tennis rackets because the pupils had raised a lot of money. All the pupils were allowed to try them out. b) If you keep your fingers crossed, perhaps I'll (I might) score 15 points. c) The Millers can't afford to make a trip because they are out of work and very short of money. d) You must not expect

18

to be alone if you go to a popular place in the country. e) The management had to sack many workers. For this reason there was a strike that the manager didn't want.

3. Schulaufgabe

1.

a) met, invited, had seen, went, talked, danced, was, said, was, drink, will lose, answered, will eat

2.

a) Must safety-belts be put on all the time? b) Can(May) radios be played during the flight?

3.

a) will, will be able to, needn't, can, is allowed to, must, might, have got to

4.

a) Watches are wrapped in paper by smugglers. b) A bottle of whisky is hidden in his luggage by a passenger. c) He might be caught and punished by the police. d) The oranges are cut in halves and stuck together again. e) The box was taken and loaded on a van.

5.

a) Why were the passengers not allowed to bring flowers to England? b) Where did one passenger hide cigarettes? c) What did the officers check very carefully? d) Whose job is not always as exciting as many people think?

4. Schulaufgabe

1.

are going to have, Should / Shall, will come, go, will be, would not have asked, had known, is playing, 'll ring, will bring, had thought, would have bought

2.

a) on, more seriously b) less expensively, least c) badly, worse, latest

3.

each other, themselves, each other, herself, himself

4.

a) had had, would have happened b) would not have found, had taken c) had shut, would not have been able to get d) would have watched, had known e) would not have seen, had hidden f) had called, have caught g) would not be, had not been

5. Schulaufgabe

1.

a) doesn't work, South-west London, works, South-east London b) he didn't get a job at BTY Computers, got a job at Digital Computers c) didn't phone for the police, he phoned for the doctor. d) she didn't lay the table, John laid the table e) he didn't drive to the supermarket in his father's car, he rode on his bike.

2.

a) when he is going to the supermarket b) that he is going in ten minutes and that he wants to write a list. c) if he is walking or going by bike. d) he is taking his bike. e) if he wants to buy some oranges.

3.

a) lives, doesn't work b) moved, had not found c) have been, for d) started, did not go, was e) will buy

4.

still, for, soon, ago, some, every, any, lots of, any, some, ones

6. Schulaufgabe

1.

of sitting, of visiting, visiting, on looking at, in seeing, walking, going, leaving, leaving, at telling, to shooting, coming, about going

2.

a) girls' b) women's c) boys' d) men's e) children's

3.

a) themselves b) each other c) each other d) herself e) each other f) himself

4.

a) good, hardest b) more often c) more nervously d) (more) carefully e) least interesting, better f) faster

7. Schulaufgabe

1.

a) colder b) worst c) most beautiful d) easiest

2.

a) lay, lain, liegen b) to lean, leant, lehnen c) to think, thought, denken d) to blow, blew, blown e) brought, brought, bringen f) to fly, flown, fliegen g) to find, found, found h) to lose, lost, verlieren

3.

a) if the telephone was ringing. b) that she had to tell him about it. c) if he could light all the candles he could find. d) that they would come to the hotel the day after. e) that she took (had taken) the prescription to the chemist's the day before.

4.

a) "Can't you come earlier, Judy?" b) "Have you lost anything, Mr Hopkins?" c) "I was never late last year."

5.

a) Hotel rooms will be booked very early. b) A big new freezer has just been put in. c) The letters must be answered by the secretaries today. d) The heating was being installed in the kitchen.

6.

a) Yesterday my father told me that he had flown to Glasgow 13 years ago. b) He said that because of a power failure in the plane, suddenly all lights had gone out. c) The crew told us to keep quiet and did everything to find the cause at once.

8. Schulaufgabe

1.

a) is used every day. b) are played here at the weekend. c) was built last year. d) was opened by G.K. e) drinks were given to each customer. f) of people will be invited next week. g) won't be left out. h) car should be checked before their holiday. i) ought to be taken to the garage. j) must be put in the tank before they start.

2.

a) After the Torrey Canyon disaster a lot of people were afraid of losing their jobs. b) Not only the fishermen were in danger of earning no money. c) Tourists were not interested in spending a holiday in Cornwall. d) A lot of them preferred going to the Scottish Highlands, instead of swimming in oil slicks. e) The people of Cornwall suggested cleaning the beaches. f) The government thought of spraying detergent. g) Everybody was looking forward to having clean beaches again.

3.

a) Du solltest (eigentlich) den neuen Film sehen, Petra. Du solltest ihn nicht versäumen. b) Du darfst auf diesem Weg nicht Rad fahren, Rachel. Du kannst dein Rad schieben. c) Tom musste seinen Eltern gestern helfen. Er muss ihnen nächsten Samstag wieder helfen. d) Johnny konnte gestern nicht ins Training kommen. Er hofft, dass er nächste Woche spielen kann. e) Mary durfte die Kamera ihres Vaters nicht benutzen. Sie muss morgen fragen. f) Hast du meinen Füller gesehen? – Er ist vielleicht in der Schublade.

9. Schulaufgabe

1.

a) Judy said that she was late and that she was very sorry. b) Mr H. asked if she had forgotten what he had said to her the day before. c) Judy answered that she hadn't and that there was something she had to tell him. d) Mr H. said that he had no time to listen to her excuses that day. e) Mr H. added that he would write a letter to her father the day after. f) Ten minutes later Mr W. asked Mr H. if he had lost his wallet that morning. g) Mr W. added that J.B. found (had found) it an hour before.

2.

a) to b) in c) at d) at(for) e) to f) about

3.

a) "Do not leave your seats." b) "Can you bring back the book next week, John?" c) "I was late yesterday because of the bad weather".

4.

a) Mrs H. was a teacher. The day she was looking forward to most, was Saturday because on Saturday there was no school. b) Last autumn she went to town by underground to buy a new fridge at last. c) The shop near where she got off, had just opened. It was about 3 o'clock/p.m. d) The man who served her said that fridges were very expensive at the moment. e) But Mrs H. said that she didn't mind. f) The shop-assistant had asked her if she knew that she had to pay the fridge straight-away.

10. Schulaufgabe

1.
a) if he had got a room. b) that it was his turn to buy some drinks. c) that somebody had taken his money. d) that he'd never got any money when it was his turn to pay. e) if he had got a cock, where it was. f) to lock the doors. g) that they would turn off the lights in a minute, he would stand there by the table. h) that everybody in the room had to come up. i) that their hands were black, his were clean.

2.
a) wouldn't have spent b) will crow c) would not be able to run away d) had not rubbed e) would have happened

3.
a) The landlord asked Tom a question. b) A landlord is someone who owns a pub. c) John MacIntosh showed Tom his right hand.

4.
a) in buying b) of showing c) on travelling d) of flying e) forward to lying f) of spending g) of riding, in, of breaking h) of booking i) of learning j) After arriving

past

present perfect

3. Schulaufgabe aus dem Englischen

3.

**Fill in the following auxiliaries (= modals), but use each only once.
Make sure you use the ríght tense.**

> will – needn't – can – be allowed to – might – be able to – have got to – must

In a few weeks it is holiday time in Britain. I'm sure there _____

be a lot of traffic on the roads, because many families are going to go on outings

in their cars. In Wales you _____

find many places in the country or in the mountains. But you _____

go so far away to escape the traffic noise: There are quiet parks in every town, where

you _____ be in a few minutes.

Of course nobody _____ make a fire there, and

also mind that people _____ follow the signs. Take an

umbrella, because it _____ rain. In England you never know!

In many British towns the parks are closed at 10 o'clock, so people

_____ leave before. What a pity!

3. Schulaufgabe aus dem Englischen

4.
Put the following sentences into the passive.

a) Smugglers wrap watches in paper.

_____

b) A passenger hides a bottle of whisky in his luggage.

_____

c) The police might catch and punish him.

_____

d) Somebody cuts the oranges in halves and sticks them together again.

_____

e) He took the box and loaded it on a van.

_____

5.
Ask questions.

a) The passengers were not allowed to bring flowers to England. (Why?)

_____

b) One passenger hid cigarettes under his shirt. (Where?)

_____

c) The officers checked the luggage very carefully. (What?)

_____

d) A pilot's job is not always as exciting as many people think. (Whose?)

_____

4. Schulaufgabe aus dem Englischen

● vermischte Zeiten   ● Adjektiv/Adverb   ● Reflexivpronomen /
● Bedingungssätze   reziproke Pronomen

1.
Fill in the correct tense.

Jeff and Lucy (have) _____ a picnic next Saturday.

They have already planned everything and bought the things they need.
Now they only have to invite some friends.

Jeff: _____ (be) I invite Tom and Frank, two of my classmates?
            What's your opinion, Lucy?

Lucy: Yes, do that. Jenny and Liz (come) _____ as well.

            I invited them yesterday. If your two friends (go) _____

            with us, there (be) _____ three girls and three boys.

Jeff: Well, you know, there's a problem: Jenny and Liz are always a bit cheeky
            to Tom and Frank, because they don't like them.

Lucy: Oh, sorry, I (not ask) _____ these two

            girls if I (know) _____ that. And Sarah can't come

            because she (play) _____ tennis on Saturday. But Linda

            can. Wait a moment. I (ring) _____ her up.

Jeff: O. K. But then there will be only five, and we need somebody else.

Lucy: Don't worry. Linda (bring) _____ her big dog with
            her. She never wants to leave it alone.

Jeff: That's very nice. If I (think) _____ of that,

            I (buy) _____ some dog food yesterday.

4. Schulaufgabe aus dem Englischen

2.
Fill in what's missing.

a) Jack is very keen _____ maths. He works (serious)

_____ at it than the other boys in his class.

b) Mr Miller has bought his car for £ 7000 and Mr Jackson for £ 8000.

Mr Miller has bought his car (expensive) _____
than Mr Jackson.
Mr Brown has only paid £ 6500 for his car. He has paid _____ of all.

c) Boss to worker: "In my opinion you work very (bad) _____,

much (bad) _____

than the others. In the morning you always arrive (late) _____
of all.

3.
Fill in the pronouns.

Danny and Evelyn like _____ very much.

They never spend money on _____.

They buy _____ presents almost every day.

Evelyn always makes _____ pretty for Danny.

Danny always looks at _____ in the mirror.

4. Schulaufgabe aus dem Englischen

4.

Complete the following sentences.

When the Blakes got home after their holidays, they found that somebody had got into their house and stolen a lot of things. Mr Blake was very upset:

a) "If we _____ a dog, nothing _____

_____ (have, happen)

b) The thieves _____ any money if we

_____ it to the bank before the holiday. (not find, take)

c) If we _____ the bathroom window, the thieves _____

_____ into the house. (shut, not be able to get)

d) Our neighbours _____ the house if they

_____ that we were not at home. (watch, know)

e) The thieves _____ our diamonds if we

_____ them more carefully. (not see, hide)

f) If our neighbours _____ the police at once,

they might _____ the thieves. (call, catch)

g) I _____ so angry if our holidays

_____ so disappointing. (not be, not be)

171

5. Schulaufgabe aus dem Englischen

● Verneinung ● indirekte Rede ● vermischte Zeiten

The Cooper family

The Coopers live in Windsor, a small town near London. Mr Cooper works in South-east London where he got a job at Digital Computers. Mrs Cooper is a secretary, but she doesn't go to her office every day. She's got enough housework to do at home. The Coopers have a new detached house with a garage and a large garden around it. The house is very convenient because it's near the school. The children are Barbara and John. Barbara is twelve, but John is only six. There is a playground behind the school, and the children usually spend the whole afternoon there.

But last week everything was different: Mrs Cooper was ill and stayed in bed. Bad luck for her! She had a dreadful headache and her husband phoned for the doctor.

When the children came home from school at half past three they wanted to help their mother. Barbara washed up in the kitchen, tidied the living-room with the vacuum cleaner, and made the tea. John laid the table and did the shopping. He wrote a long list before he rode to the supermarket on his bike. He took his calculator with him. Do you know why? He wanted to see if the cashier at the check-out made a mistake. "When my mother is ill in bed, I must see that everything is all right," he said to his sister.

1.
Correct the sentences.

a) Mr Cooper works in South-west London.

No, he _____ in _____

He _____ in _____

b) He got a job at BTY Computers.

No, _____

He _____

5. Schulaufgabe aus dem Englischen

c) Mrs Cooper's husband phoned for the police.

No, _____

_____

d) Barbara laid the table.

No, _____

_____

e) John drove to the supermarket in his father's car.

No, _____

_____

2.
John and his mother are talking about the shopping list.
Give a report.

a) Mother: "When are you going to the supermarket?"

Mother asks John _____

b) John: "I'm going in ten minutes. I want to write a list."

John answers _____

_____

c) Mother: "Are you walking or going by bike?"

Mother wants to know _____

d) John: "I'm taking my bike."

John says _____

e) Mother: "Do you want to buy some oranges?"

Mother asks John _____

5. Schulaufgabe aus dem Englischen

3.
Fill in the correct tense form of the verbs given in brackets.

a) Mr Cooper _____ (live) in Windsor, but he _____
   (not/work) there.

b) The Coopers _____ (move) to Windsor last year because

   Mr Cooper _____ (not/find) a job in his home
   town.

c) They _____ (be) in their new house _____
   (for/since?) ten months now.

d) Barbara _____ (start) school in Windsor last September, but

   John _____ (not/go) to school then because he

   _____ (be) only four years old.

e) Mr Cooper _____ (buy) a new car next summer.

4.
One week later Mrs Cooper has written a letter.

Fill in: ago – any – any – every – for – lots of – never – one – ones – some – some – soon – still – yet. (Odd words out!)

I'm _____ in bed. I've been ill _____ over a week now.

I hope I'll feel better _____. The doctor came two days _____

and he gave me _____ pills. John goes shopping _____ day. There

isn't _____ food left and so he buys _____ things. He didn't buy

_____ pears, but he got _____ apples. I like the sweet _____ very much.

174

6. Schulaufgabe aus dem Englischen

● Gerund   ● s-Genitiv   ● Reflexivpronomen
● Adjektiv/Adverb

1.

Fill in the correct forms of the following verbs and prepositions, where necessary.
(look at, see, go 2x, sit, leave 2x, shoot, walk, tell, visit 2x, come)

One afternoon the Traynors were all sitting in the living room.

"Instead _____ in front of the TV all afternoon

we could go on a short sightseeing tour and visit the town museum", said Mr Traynor.

"I've thought _____ it for a long time."

"Oh, yes", answered Paul. "Thats's a good idea. I really enjoy _____

_____ museums. I'm especially keen _____

old guns."

Jean said: "I'm interested _____

old pictures." Mrs Traynor always prefers _____ to

_____ by car, so she said: "I suggest _____

the car at home." Before _____ the house they had a cup of

tea. Then they went to the museum where a guide showed them round. He was

good _____ stories. Paul was looking forward

_____ with an old gun. After _____

home they had a wonderful meal and talked _____

there again.

175

6. Schulaufgabe aus dem Englischen

2.
Use the possessive forms for the underlined expressions.

Paul and Jean went to a department store. They saw a lot of things there: dresses <u>for girls</u>, hats <u>for women</u>, bicycles <u>for boys</u>, coats <u>for men</u>, shoes <u>for children</u>

a) _____ dresses   b) _____ hats,

c) _____ bicycles,   d) _____ coats,

e) _____ shoes.

3.
Fill in a reflexive pronoun or each other.

a) Jane and Paul enjoyed _____ very much at the museum.

b) They often go out together, because they like _____ very much.

c) At school they sit next to _____.

d) Jane can't stop talking when she is alone.

   She often talks to _____.

e) Sometimes they have an argument with _____.

f) Paul asked _____ why Jane was angry last night.

6. Schulaufgabe aus dem Englischen

4.
Fill in the correct forms.

a) Jane got a _____ result in the English exam,

because she had worked _____ of all the pupils
in the class.   (good, hard)

b) Mac won the shooting contest in his club last weekend.

He hit the target _____ than everybody else.   (often)

c) Paul worked _____ in his maths test
than all the other boys.   (nervous)

d) He'll have to work _____ in future or
he will stay down.   (careful)

e) German is the _____ language for Jane.

She doesn't like it very much. She likes French _____
than any other subject.   (interesting, good)

f) Paul often comes to school by bike, because it's _____.
(fast)

7. Schulaufgabe aus dem Englischen

- Steigerung
- direkte Rede
- unregelmäßige Verben
- Passiv
- indirekte Rede

1.
Find opposites for the underlined words.

a) Last summer August was <u>hotter</u> than the year before.

_____

b) Sport is Bob's <u>best</u> subject at school.

_____

c) This is the <u>ugliest</u> picture I've ever seen.

_____

d) The <u>most difficult</u> way to cross the river is to jump over it.

_____

2.
Irregular verbs.

a) to lie   _____   _____   _____

b) _____   leant   _____   _____

c) _____   _____   thought   _____

d) _____   _____   _____   blasen

e) to bring   _____   _____   _____

f) _____   flew   _____   _____

g) _____   _____   _____   finden

h) _____   _____   lost   _____

178

7. Schulaufgabe aus dem Englischen

3.
Put into reported speech.

a) Reporter: "Is the telephone ringing?"

The reporter asked _____

b) Sally: "Sue, you must tell him about it."

Sally told Sue _____

c) Manager to waiter: "Can you light all the candles you can find?"

The manager asked the waiter _____

_____

d) The girls: "We will come to the hotel tomorrow."

The girls said _____

e) Jennifer told me last week: "I took the prescription to the chemist's yesterday."

Jennifer told me last week _____

_____

4.
Put into direct speech.

a) Mr Wilson asked Judy if she couldn't come earlier.

_____

b) The headmaster asked Mr Hopkins if he had lost anything.

_____

c) Judy's mother said that she had never been late the year before.

_____

7. Schulaufgabe aus dem Englischen

5.
Put into the passive voice.

a) Many people will book their hotel rooms very early.

_____

b) They have just put in a big new freezer.

_____

c) The secretaries must answer the letters today.

_____

d) You were installing the heating in the kitchen.

_____

6.
Translation.

a) Gestern erzählte mir mein Vater, dass er vor 13 Jahren nach Glasgow geflogen war.

_____

_____

b) Er sagte, dass wegen eines Stromausfalls plötzlich im Flugzeug alle Lichter ausgingen.

_____

_____

c) Die Besatzung wies uns an Ruhe zu bewahren und tat alles, um die Ursache sofort zu finden.

_____

_____

8. Schulaufgabe aus dem Englischen

● Passiv   ● Gerund   ● modale Hilfsverben

1.
Re-write the following sentences. Don't change the meaning.

a) They use the sports field every day.

The sports field _____

b) They play games here at the weekend.

Games _____

c) They built the supermarket last year.

It _____

d) Geoffrey Knickerbocker opened it.

It _____

e) They gave free drinks to each customer.

Free _____

f) They will invite lots of people next week.

Lots _____

g) They won't leave you out.

You _____

h) They should check the car before their holiday.

The _____

i) They ought to take it to the garage.

It _____

j) They must put petrol in the tank before they start.

Petrol _____

8. Schulaufgabe aus dem Englischen

2.
Form complete sentences using the gerund and past tense.

a) After the Torrey Canyon disaster / a lot of people / afraid / lose / jobs

_____

_____

b) Not only the fishermen / in danger / earn / no money

_____

_____

c) Tourists / not interested / spend / holiday in Cornwall

_____

_____

d) A lot of them / prefer / go / Scottish Highlands / instead / swim / in oil slicks

_____

_____

e) The people of Cornwall / suggest / clean / beaches

_____

_____

f) The government / think / spray / detergent

_____

_____

g) Everybody / look forward / have / clean beaches again

_____

8. Schulaufgabe aus dem Englischen

3.
Translation.

a) You ought to see the new film, Petra. You oughtn't to miss it.

_____

_____

b) You mustn't cycle on this path, Rachel. You can push your bike.

_____

_____

c) Tom had to help his parents yesterday. He'll have to help them again next Saturday.

_____

_____

d) Johnny couldn't come to training yesterday. He hopes he'll be able to play next week.

_____

_____

e) Mary wasn't allowed to use her father's camera. She'll have to ask tomorrow.

_____

_____

f) Have you seen my pen? – It may be in the drawer.

_____

_____

9. Schulaufgabe aus dem Englischen

1.

Put the following dialogue into reported speech. The reporting verb must be in the past tense.

a) Judy: "I'm late. I'm very sorry."

_____

b) Mr Hopkins: "Have you forgotten what I said to you yesterday?"

_____

_____

c) Judy: "No, I haven't. There is something I must tell you."

_____

_____

d) Mr Hopkins: "I've no time to listen to your excuses today."

_____

_____

e) Mr Hopkins: "I'll write a letter to your father tomorrow."

_____

f) Ten minutes later. Mr Wilson: "Have you lost your wallet this morning, Mr Hopkins?"

_____

_____

g) Mr Wilson: "Judy Baker found it an hour ago."

_____

9. Schulaufgabe aus dem Englischen

2.
Fill in the missing prepositions.

a) Which school do you go _____?

b) What are you interested _____?

c) Which subjects are you good_____?

d) What magazines are you looking_____?

e) Who does this house belong_____?

f) What were the girls talking _____?

3.
Put into direct speech.

a) The hijackers warned the passengers not to leave their seats.

_____

_____

b) Mrs Smith asked John if he could bring back the book the following week.

_____

_____

c) Jim said that he had been late the day before because of the bad weather.

_____

_____

9. Schulaufgabe aus dem Englischen

4.
Translation.

a) Frau Harrison war Lehrerin. Der Tag, auf den sie sich am meisten freute, war Samstag, denn samstags war keine Schule.

b) Letzten Herbst fuhr sie mit der U-Bahn in die Stadt, um endlich einen neuen Kühlschrank zu kaufen.

c) Das Kaufhaus, in dessen Nähe sie ausstieg, hatte gerade aufgemacht. Es war ungefähr 15.00 Uhr.

d) Der Mann, der sie bediente, sagte, Kühlschränke seien im Augenblick sehr teuer.

e) Aber Frau Harrison sagte, dass ihr das nichts ausmache.

f) Der Verkäufer hatte sie gefragt, ob sie wüsste, dass sie den Kühlschrank sofort bezahlen müsse.

10. Schulaufgabe aus dem Englischen

● Indirekte Rede   ● Bedingungssätze   ● Wortstellung
● Gerund

Comprehension Test

The clever cock

One cold November evening Tom O'Connor was driving through Scotland towards Aberdeen. It was late and he was tired, so he stopped in a small village at a pub. He went up to the landlord and asked: <u>"Have you got a room</u> for tonight?" The man answered 'yes'.

After some time Tom came downstairs. Some farmers were playing darts. The man who lost grinned sheepishly: <u>"It's my turn to buy some drinks.</u>" He put his hand into the pocket of his jacket, went red in the face and gabbled: <u>"Somebody's taken my money.</u>" The others laughed and one of them exclaimed: <u>"You've never got any money when it's your turn to pay</u>." But this time it was really true.

At that moment Tom got up from his chair and said to the landlord: <u>"Have you got a cock? Where is it?"</u> Though Tom's idea was ridiculous, the landlord came back with a lovely cock. Tom took the big black cooking pot from the fireplace and put the cock under the pot. <u>"Now lock the doors"</u>, he said. <u>"In a minute we'll turn off the lights. I'll stand here by the table</u>. Then <u>everybody in the room must come up</u> and rub his right hand across the bottom of the pot. If the thief does that the cock will crow."

Then one by one came up to the table and rubbed the pot. "The cock hasn't crowed yet. Has everyone rubbed the pot?" asked Tom. Nobody else moved. The lights went on. "Now show me your right hands, please." He looked at all their hands. Then he said to John MacIntosh: "Look at the others' hands, then look at yours. <u>Their hands are black, yours is clean.</u> You know why you didn't rub the pot, don't you?"

10. Schulaufgabe aus dem Englischen

1.
Put the underlined sentences into reported speech.

a) Tom wanted to know _____

b) The man who lost said _____

_____

c) Then he remarked _____

d) One of the others exclaimed _____

_____

e) Tom asked the landlord _____

and _____

f) He told them _____

g) Then he said _____

_____ and _____

_____

h) Tom demanded _____

_____

i) Tom told John Mac Intosh _____

and _____

10. Schulaufgabe aus dem Englischen

2.
Fill in the right forms of the verbs.

a) If Tom hadn't been so tired he _____

_____ (not spend) the night in the pub.

b) The cock _____ (crow) if the thief rubs the pot.

c) Tom said: "If we locked the door, the thief _____

_____ (cannot run away).

d) He told the farmers: "We wouldn't have known the thief if you _____

_____ (not rub) the pot."

e) What _____ (happen) if Tom
hadn't come into the pub?

3.
Form sentences.

a) a question / Tom / the landlord / asked

_____

b) a pub / who / a landlord / owns / someone / is

_____

c) Tom / his right hand / John MacIntosh / showed

_____

_____

10. Schulaufgabe aus dem Englischen

4.
Fill in the missing words.

In a newspaper Tom found the following advertisements:

a) Are you interested _____ (buy) a radio?

b) Give us the chance _____ (show) you
   our latest model.

c) Are you keen _____ (travel)?

d) Don't be afraid _____ (fly).

e) Are you looking _____ (lie)
   on the beach?

f) Instead _____ (spend) your holiday
   at home come to Scotland.

g) Many people dream _____ (ride) a horse,

   but you may be _____ danger _____
   (break) your bones.

h) The best way _____ (book) a holiday
   is to phone us.

i) We give you a good opportunity _____
   (learn) English in England.

j) _____ (arrive) in England, you
   will be welcomed by your host family.

Wir bringen dich weiter:

Alois Mayer

Französisch 1. Lernjahr
*Grammatik – Wortschatz –
Rechtschreibung – Fehlerquellen*

*Themen des ersten Lernjahres
werden anschaulich erläutert und
in zahlreichen Übungen gefestigt.
Eine ideale Hilfe für das selbständige
Lernen zu Hause.*

ISBN 3-7863-0707-5

Gerhard Fink

Tips – Tricks – Training Latein 1
Konjugationen ab 1. Lernjahr

*Konjugationen leicht verständlich
und amüsant erklärt und geübt.*

ISBN 3-7863-0752-0

**Über das MANZ Lernhilfen-Programm
informiert Sie Ihre Buchhandlung**

Wir bringen dich weiter:

Achim Homm

Wörterbücher sinnvoll nutzen
Erklärungen – Beispiele – Übungen

Eine gründliche und für jeden verständliche Einübung der Arbeit mit dem zweisprachigen Wörterbuch. Zahlreiche Beispiele und Übungen erleichtern das Verständnis.

ISBN 3-7863-2015-2

Werner Kieweg

Tenses – Englische Zeitformen im Überblick
Erklärungen – Beispiele – Übungen

Ein kompakter Überblick zu allen englischen Zeitformen und ihren Verwendungsmöglichkeiten sowie vielfältige Übungen dazu. Ein hilfreicher Begleiter durch die gesamte Schulzeit.

ISBN 3-7863-2036-5

Über das MANZ Lernhilfen-Programm informiert Sie Ihre Buchhandlung